NEVER CAN'T

Foreword by J. Oswald Sanders

LINNET HINTON

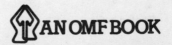

© OVERSEAS MISSIONARY FELLOWSHIP
(formerly China Inland Mission)
Published by Overseas Missionary Fellowship (IHQ) Ltd.,
2 Cluny Road, Singapore 1025,
Republic of Singapore

First published 1987

OMF BOOKS are distributed by
OMF, 404 South Church Street,
  Robesonia, Pa 19551, USA
OMF, Belmont, The Vine,
  Sevenoaks, Kent, TN13 3TZ, UK
OMF, PO Box 177, Kew East,
  Victoria 3102, Australia
and other OMF offices.

ISBN 9971-972-56-5

Printed in Singapore

CONTENTS

To my parents
whose lives have been
a consistent and winsome example
of Christian discipleship

FOREWORD

A friendship extending over fifty years that has been renewed and refurbished in several countries, is something to be cherished. It began with Norman and Amy as a student-teacher relationship, later to be followed by a director-missionary association. A memorable and hair-raising journey by jeep over the rugged mountains of North-west China into the area of Tibet where Norman and Amy later ministered, brought us into a closer fellowship which has been maintained through the years.

That is one reason why I am delighted to write a foreword to this book, which I have read with more than ordinary interest and appreciation. Considering her relationship to the subjects, the author has been remarkably successful in presenting an objective and gripping story of a most fruitful husband-wife partnership — no easy task.

This story will bring great encouragement to those who feel unsophisticated, and unprivileged in education. God has no favourites. Norman started behind scratch in these areas, but a continuing dependence on God enabled him to overtake and pass many who were more privileged. It could be said of him as it was of Emma Piechynska, wife of a sadistic Polish count, that his life was enriched by the things that were withheld. It is also true that without the gifts and dedication Amy contributed to the partnership, the story might well have been different.

In ministry around the world, without mentioning names,

I have quoted Norman as an example of one who from student days, exhibited the true servant spirit. I believe that this, more than any other single factor, was the secret of the continuing fruitfulness of their joint ministry.

Norman has emphasized that their story is but a page out of the history of the work of the Overseas Missionary Fellowship, and that what they have achieved has been through the prayers, encouragement and support of the Fellowship and many friends around the world. This is true, but it is also true that to an unusual degree they have succeeded by loving and caring ministry, in giving more than they have received.

I can foresee a widespreading ministry for this book, for the factuality of which I can vouch.

J Oswald Sanders

PREFACE

T his is the story of what God has done through the lives of two ordinary people totally committed to Him. My father was a farm labourer and my mother a primary school teacher. As a young couple, they determined that the rule for their life should be complete and unquestioning obedience to their Master, the Lord Jesus Christ.

One of my father's good friends, the late Rev. John Deane of the New Zealand Bible College, used to say to his students, "It's like climbing on to a magic carpet. When you trust your lives to God completely, and are prepared to do whatever He asks you to do, you may be transported to the ends of the earth and find yourself accomplishing things of which you never dreamed."

This has been so with my parents. The path of obedience has led them to the high grasslands of Tibet, through the green jungles of Malaya and into the congested cities of tropical Asia. They have lived through wars, been exposed to diseases and repeatedly lost their possessions. They have experienced the pain of separation and the grief of bereavement, and know what it is to be rejected, betrayed and hated for Christ's sake. They have been consistently pushed into jobs too big for them and into situations that threw them into utter dependence upon God.

But through it all they have known the presence of the Master, guiding and sustaining them. In times of extremity, they have received from His hand most wonderful, even miraculous, provisions. When stretched beyond endurance, they have drawn on that strength which shows more completely in times of weakness and have not been disappointed. Through the Holy Spirit, they have known victory over fear and comfort in sorrow. To their great joy, God has through them delivered many people from the power of darkness and inspired many others to a life of full consecration to Himself.

Painfully aware of their own inadequacies, faults and failures, they gratefully attribute all that has been achieved to the grace of God, and would underscore Paul's words in 2 Corinthians 4:7 — "But we have this treasure (the knowledge and presence of God) in jars of clay to show that this all-surpassing power is from God and not from us." They have never ceased to be amazed at what God has graciously done for them, in them, and through them. To God be the glory!

This is, by rights, my mother's book. She was the one who sifted through the memorabilia of a lifetime and put together the first manuscript, primarily in response to the oft-repeated request from family members to "Tell us about your life. We want to know!" Fortunately, Mother Lascelles had kept all their letters which was a great aid to memory.

Mine has been the pleasurable task of pulling it all into a book. There was pain as well. So much had to be left out, and every time I had to amputate a good story from the original manuscript, I bled! But I believe this abbreviated version of their history still carries the clear message that God delights to use ordinary men and women in His service, that He gives the power to do what He commands, and that He is unfailingly faithful to those who trust and obey Him.

Linnet S Hinton
September 1986

A young couple stood in a quiet corner of the sunny garden engrossed in conversation. They were members of a team running a children's mission at a popular seaside resort. The busy days left little opportunity for private meetings but, in a brief respite between activities, these two found a few moments to be alone.

They were soon to become engaged. As they looked into each other's eyes, the cries of seagulls circling overhead and the shrill voices of children playing on the beach faded into the distance. During the previous few months they had seen very little of one another. This time was very precious.

As they anticipated life together in the service of God, there were many things to plan. This particular afternoon, they were discussing the implications of the Christian life. The "life of faith," what did it really mean?

"If we honestly believe," said the young man earnestly, "that nothing is impossible to God and that we can do anything with His help, then we can never say 'I can't' when He asks us to do something."

"No," assented his partner, "it would be casting a slur on His ability, wouldn't it?"

"God has given us so many promises to assure us that He will enable us if we obey Him," went on the young man. After a thoughtful pause, he added, "If we say 'I can't,' we make His promise untrue."

In all seriousness, this 23-year-old couple agreed that the

word "can't" should be struck out of their vocabulary. It is not a word for those whom God is calling to work with Him.

The young man fished a piece of paper out of his pocket and, with his pencil, wrote CAN'T in large letters. Then, very solemnly, for they were both in deadly earnest, he dug a hole in the garden and buried the paper.

"By God's grace," they covenanted, "we will never say 'can't' when He asks us to do anything!"

And they meant it. It was an act of faith. As they looked towards an unknown future in a foreign land, they determined on this rule for their lives — implicit, unquestioning obedience to the will of God, the One who can be trusted.

"What is obedience after all," they concluded, "but faith in action?"

What had brought these two young adults to this point in their lives and where were they going?

CHAPTER I

FREED TO LIVE

Distant snow-capped mountains glistened against a deep blue sky. The rugged, tussock-covered hills of the high country gave way in turn to rolling downs and green pastures dotted with sheep. A great stillness lay over the land. Even the gentle rattle of harness as the horse cropped grass nearby, seemed to be swallowed up in silence.

The light and peace of the scene contrasted strongly with the dark turmoil of spirit in the heart of the young shepherd who was out there alone mending the boundary fence. At nineteen years of age, Norman McIntosh was disappointed with life, frustrated with himself and tormented by a haunting sense of guilt. He had been in this state of mind now for two miserable years. Once again his thoughts churned endlessly around the well-worn grooves. Was there no way out of this trap of unhappiness?

It was 1931 and the effects of the Great Depression were being increasingly felt in rural New Zealand. Many businesses were hard pressed, including that of the carpenter-builder in Timaru to whom Norman had been apprenticed. Because he liked and respected his employer, Norman decided to make things easier for him by voluntarily breaking his bond. Also, he had to admit, it was a relief to get out of a job he hadn't really enjoyed. Sheer necessity had determined he take up carpentry, the only avenue of training open to him. His time in the trade had, however, given him an appreciative feel for wood and a useful practical skill.

For a while after leaving the city, he subsisted on various odd farm jobs until he was fortunate enough to find more permanent work through an unemployment relief scheme. He ended up at Ashby's sheep station in Gapes Valley. The hours were long, often from six in the morning until nine at night, and the pay a pittance, but at least he had his keep.

Secretly he longed to be a doctor. *But what a stupid, impossible dream for a pauper like me*, he thought. *You have to be rich to be a doctor.*

In his family it had always been a struggle just to keep everyone fed and clothed. Norman had been born in Wyndham, Southland, where his father, Henry McIntosh, was a farmhand. Three other children had followed him in quick succession.

Then suddenly, when he was five, his mother had fallen ill. He could still hear her weak voice calling from the bed, "Son, you'll have to be a big boy now and help Mummy. I can't get up. Do you think you could bath Ruby for me?"

Frightened and confused, he hauled the heavy tin tub to her bedside. Then, as she encouraged him, made what seemed endless trips back and forth from the kitchen carrying warm water in a jug. Somehow he managed to wrestle the baby into the tub and out again, but she kicked and howled the whole time and water splashed all over the floor.

A few days later his mother, Emily Nutsford McIntosh, aged only 27 had died. There was no cure for peritonitis in those days.

Kindly neighbours helped where they could, but the months after his wife's death were extremely difficult for the young man so suddenly left with the sole care of four small children. Not for the first time, Norman wondered, *Is this when Dad started drinking more heavily?* Through the years his father's growing problem with alcohol had sadly compounded the difficulties in the home.

Up in the hills that afternoon, Norman was oblivious to the beauty around him as one memory crowded in on the next. Vividly he recalled a night soon after his mother's death. He had woken in alarm when his father snatched him from his bed. The house was ablaze, the flames already racing out of control by the time Henry rushed with his children to safety across the paddock. Far out in the country, there was no way to fight the fire, and they could only watch helplessly as everything they owned was reduced to cinders. Just the chimney was left standing.

After this double calamity, Henry decided to make a new start. In search of work he moved north into South Canterbury, eventually finding a job as a teamster in the hamlet of Woodbury. Their nearest town, Geraldine, was seven miles away. A series of dreadful housekeepers pre-ceeded Henry's remarriage to Barbara Gulskoskie, a widow with two teenage children. She earned her living as a midwife and was known and loved throughout the district. Barbara was a simple but practical person, generous and affectionate, and she loved her four stepchildren and gave them a stable, happy home and family life.

It was while Norman was at primary school in Woodbury that the McIntoshes, along with so many others, began to feel the pinch of poverty more cruelly. Henry and Barbara shielded their children as much as possible by their love and hard work but the young ones had to play their part in making ends meet. Until they were old enough to have weekend jobs, they had to spend their Saturdays and holidays pulling prickly gorse and broom sticks from the river bed and dragging them home for firewood. Eels and rabbits often provided meals during those lean years and, although the children didn't always understand why, they learned to do without many of the things other youngsters took for granted.

Norman, being the oldest, had to shoulder responsibility beyond his years. His day started at five o'clock when he got up to kindle the fire in preparation for breakfast. Then the horse had to be fetched, fed and saddled ready for his father to ride to work. Two cows also had to be brought in and milked before he went off to school.

In spite of their poverty, his parents insisted that each of

their children have the opportunity of a high school education. For Norman this meant a fourteen-mile bicycle ride
each day to and from the Geraldine District High School. The
journey into town wasn't so bad, but the homeward ride was
uphill all the way and often he had to pedal against a stiff
nor'west wind as well. On such days he would arrive home
worn out. Also, the shingle roads could be hazardous. Once
when his bike skidded sharply, he was thrown off and broke a
leg. This was a major disaster for a family that lived so close to
the breadline. Deep gloom descended on the home. The
doctor had to be called all the way from Geraldine and his
repeated visits ran up a medical bill that took proud but
honest Henry a long time to pay off.

It was necessary for Norman to spend his Saturdays
working — mowing lawns, gardening, milking cows —
anything that would bring in a few shillings. He had to save
up to purchase his own bike and pay for other school
expenses.

Like all teenagers he hankered to be the same as everyone
else, and was acutely embarrassed at having to wear
secondhand clothing. His thrifty stepmother skilfully made
and turned clothing for her family as there was never any
money for buying new and ready-made. But how Norman
suffered in his homemade garments. He tortured himself with
what he imagined his classmates were saying behind his back.
Perhaps he'd been overly sensitive, but he still cringed when
he remembered a certain overcoat.

One day the people for whom his father worked, rather
aristocratic and kindly folk who often helped them in this
way, gave them a used naval officer's uniform coat. It was
made of beautiful material but had an old-fashioned astrakhan
collar. Norman's mother carefully cut this down and recon-
structed an overcoat for him which was warm and adequate
but patently homemade and different, especially with its
lamb's wool collar. Norman went through such agonies
because of it that every day he would take the wretched thing
off a mile out of town and roll it up on the carrier of his cycle.

He would arrive at school wet and shivering rather than face the fancied ridicule of his fellows.

As a carpenter's apprentice he had earned fifteen shillings a week but his board was twenty shillings, a week, and he still had to depend on his father for the extra five shillings to make up the amount. Now at Gapes Valley, on 7/6 a week, he was too poor to buy even a pair of shoelaces. He resorted to purchasing one lace at a time and cutting it in half!

If only there had been more money, he thought moodily for the thousandth time, *I might have had the chance to be somebody, to accomplish something. But here I am, a half-trained carpenter, an odd-job man, qualified for nothing, going nowhere.*

Norman had, in fact, a great deal of unrealized ability. Like many Scots, he had a solid respect for learning and had worked hard at high school, coming top of his class in his last year. But shortness of funds had limited his time there to only three years. All his life he lamented his truncated schooling and never really rid himself of the notion that he'd have been a better man if he'd "had a university education."

He was painfully shy and sensitive. After a social encounter when he felt he'd bungled, he would burn with the recollection of how awkward and tongue-tied he'd been. Perhaps, if he'd shown up better at sports he might have gained the acclaim for which his lonely spirit hungered. He loved games but wasn't very adept, and when teams were made up, he'd be left until last or overlooked altogether. Then he'd show off and play practical jokes in an effort to get attention. All in all, he was fed up with himself!

Here we go again, he muttered as he strained at a fence wire. *If we hadn't lived so far away and I'd not had to work in the weekends, I might have got into more out-of-school activities, probably made more friends. I always seem to be on the fringe of things.*

Not surprisingly, books and the dream world early became his greatest satisfaction and way of escape. His father was an intelligent man who relished books and thoughtful conversation. Norman cherished the memories of those evenings when, after the rest of the family had retired to bed, he and his dad would share the dying fire together. Then Henry would speak of books and discuss current issues. His son hadn't always understood it all, but those sessions taught him to think and planted in his young mind a love for reading and good literature. When the village library closed down, several shelves of unread classics were offered for sale at threepence a copy. "It's a bargain, son! Buy them and read them!" Norman's father had urged.

In the classroom, new vistas opened to the lad through drama, literature and poetry. He was always grateful to Dorothy Farnie, the principal, who also taught him to love and appreciate good music. Twice a day, as the students filed into their classrooms and sat at their desks, she played a record of classical music, accompanying it with a brief explanation about the composer, orchestra or artist. Listening to fine music was ever afterwards an exquisite pleasure to this young man who, although he loved to sing, was somewhat tone deaf and found it difficult to carry a tune on his own.

Out at the boundary fence that golden afternoon, however, he felt like a grub, unloved and unlovely, yet frustrated by a dim consciousness that a butterfly was trapped within. Oh, how could he be set free? Then his thoughts took another tack. . .

There had been no Christian influence in his home in the early years. His father, in softened moods or stimulated by alcohol, spoke of and often sung songs and choruses from the Torrey-Alexander mission held in Melbourne in his youth. But he always scoffed at the church and and professed to despise all "men of the cloth." Norman's own mother, whom he scarcely remembered, had been a true Christian. This he discovered only years later when somebody showed him an autograph book in which she had written some lines that bore clear testimony of her personal faith.

It wasn't until the family moved to Canterbury, however, that there was any positive Christian input. Robert Morrison, owner-manager of a large general store in Geraldine, was a stalwart in the Brethren Assembly. He was devoted to his Lord and had a great love for boys and girls. For forty years he travelled to Woodbury every Sunday afternoon to conduct a Sunday School class in the local school building.

Soon after arriving in the district, Henry was making some purchases at Morrison Bros. when he was spotted as a stranger by the manager. In his typical, kindly fashion, Bob Morrison started to chat with him.

"You a newcomer to the area?" he inquired. When Henry admitted he was, he asked, "Got any children?"

"Four," was the reply.

"What about sending them to Sunday School next week?" he asked. This surprising invitation, being offered in such a friendly way and by one of the most influential men in the district, disarmed Henry who would normally have rejected such a suggestion with hostility.

Norman recalled wryly how the four of them were scrubbed up each Sunday afternoon, dressed in their best clothes and sent off to Sunday School. There, from the lips of a man whose face glowed with his love for the Saviour, Norman first heard the gospel. Bob Morrison's students learned two things very clearly. They were sinners and they needed to be born again.

What Norman heard took only unconscious root in his mind at the time. But during his high school days he began to feel an inner yearning for God and for salvation; so much so that he became increasingly uneasy with some of the talk and activities in which his contemporaries indulged.

Later, during his years of apprenticeship in the city of Timaru, he used to attend night classes in architectural drawing. After class he would sometimes go out on the town with the other youths. They would wander about in a gang, smoking, showing off, following the girls with annoying comments and raucous laughter. There'd be drink too, though Norman would never touch the stuff because of the sorrow it had brought into his own home. He'd arrive back at his lodgings in the early hours of the morning.

Then he would hear a small Voice in his soul, saying, "Yes, you've had a great time tonight, haven't you? But remember, you're a sinner and you need to be born again!"

On one occasion, the struggle in his heart was so intense that he overcame his shyness and called on a minister to ask about "joining the church." Here was a person in deep spiritual need, but the minister missed his cue. "Oh," he said jovially, "Come along and meet the young people ... join the tennis club ...!" Norman shrank away, never to return. He realized that this man could not help him.

Another night, on his way through town, he was attracted by a light shining from the doorway of a hall. When he looked in, he saw a picture projected on a screen. An elderly man was showing lantern slides. Because the night was cold, and his curiosity was piqued, Norman crept into the darkened hall. Immediately, someone shut the door behind him!

With a group of his peers, Norman might have acted big and brave, but isolated in a strange hall he lacked the courage to turn the door handle and walk out. So he stayed.

The speaker, Mr Alex Mill of the Egypt General Mission, was pleading for a young man to take the gospel to the Bedouin Arabs. He said that night after night he had travelled up and down New Zealand with this challenge and not one young man had responded.

Again Norman heard that Voice within.

"You could do that — you are young and free. But you don't know Me yet. You are a sinner and you need to be born again!"

He had left the city, taking his unhappiness with him. Now, high up in the lonely hills, the same battle raged on in his heart. Underlying all his personal frustrations and disappointments was this ever-deepening conviction of sin.

The Voice thundered in the silence, "You are a sinner! You are guilty!"

Suddenly he could bear it no longer. He flung down his maul, grabbed his horse and hurried down to the hut where he had been living alone. He knew there was a Bible in his trunk. In desperation he drew it out and threw it on the bunk. Amazingly, it opened at Romans chapter five. Completely broken, Norman knelt down and read from verse one, "Therefore, being justified by faith, we have peace with God through our Lord Jesus Christ." Peace, oh for peace!

That day a great miracle took place in Norman's life. He cried out to the Lord and was heard. In humble confession and faith, he accepted Christ to be his Saviour, and knew God's forgiveness. He declared later that he also had the sense of taking himself in his hands, as it were, and offering himself to God for service, totally, unconditionally and forever.

The battle was over. The simple shepherd's hut seemed full of the glory of the Lord as Norman experienced the joy of being accepted by God and realized in his soul the sweetness of being at peace with God.

In his own eyes and possibly in the eyes of others, he was of little importance or value in the world. But in the eyes of the Lord he was very precious. Somehow Norman knew himself to be truly and deeply loved and valued.

From the moment when he yielded himself so completely to God, the rich potential of his life began to be realized. His spirit was set free and all the subsequent flowering of personality and ability that followed grew out of this, to his own never-ending amazement and to the glory of his Saviour.

While he was altogether unconscious of it, and long before his conversion, God had been at work in his life. His Christian mother, before her premature death, had surely prayed for her infant son. From his primary school days he had known the gospel and been followed by the prayers of God's faithful servant, Bob Morrison.

The very poverty which he so deplored and resented had been used by God to build character and to protect His child from moral harm. If he had not been so hamstrung by lack of means, Norman, who craved the friendship of his fellows, would have plunged more fully into the social life of the district and this could easily have chilled the stirrings of God's Spirit on his soul. Isolation was one of the means through which God drew this young man to Himself. Poverty had also developed in him a capacity for hard work and powers of endurance which were to stand him in good stead in the strenuous years ahead.

With joyful anticipation, Norman became aware that he had a future after all, a future that beckoned, a future full of limitless possibilities.

T wo days after his conversion, Norman took his horse and rode down to Geraldine to see Bob Morrison. As he entered the manager's office, Mr Morrison looked up and exclaimed, "No need to tell me! I know what's happened! I can see it in your face! Praise God!"

It was a joyful visit. As Norman was about to leave, this wise man pulled a volume from his bookcase and handed it to him. "Take this along with you," he said. "My eyes aren't too good now for reading."

The book was a biography, *George Muller of Bristol* by A T Pierson. Back in his lodgings that night, Norman read it avidly. Readily he identified with the young George Muller who, a century before and at a similar age, had experienced the wonderful, life-changing grace of God. He too had responded by ardently offering himself for the service of the Saviour.

George Muller was eventually used by God to care for some ten thousand orphans, without any humanly guaranteed financial backing. In the process, he became a living demonstration to the Christian world that God is faithful to His Word and that His children can utterly depend upon Him. As he read, Norman was deeply moved. Several things influenced him profoundly.

Muller revered the Scriptures as God's Word. It was his habit to turn to his Bible daily "under the double impulse of duty and delight." Meditatively and prayerfully he searched the Scriptures, then immediately and courageously he turned what he learned into practical obedience. Consequently he developed the most intimate knowledge of God.

With God's help, decided Norman as he extinguished the candle and rolled over to sleep, *I will read my Bible like this first thing tomorrow morning, and every morning!* From that day on he tried to keep sacred for God the first hour of every day.

Norman was always grateful for the necessity that had forced him, in childhood, to develop the habit of early rising. Through the years, these dawn hours have been the mainspring of his life. Like Muller, he too developed a listening ear and an obedient heart and found his love for the Master constantly renewed and deepened. In later years we children got used to having Dad emerge from his devotions brimming over with some new insight he had been given from the Word. This close fellowship with God has resulted in a life that has been evergreen, "like a tree planted by streams of water, which yields its fruit in season and whose leaf does not wither. Whatever he does prospers" (Psalm 1:3).

Muller depended upon God alone to meet his needs. As newly-weds, he and his wife were prompted by the Spirit to give away everything they possessed. From then on, until the day they died, as Muller's biographer puts it, "they were put to ample daily test both in their faith in the Great Provider and the faithfulness of the Great Promiser." Muller firmly believed that "only by *using* faith are we kept from practically *losing* it, and, on the contrary, to use faith is to lose the unbelief that hinders God's mighty acts." He determined to keep himself in that state of complete dependence where faith had to be exercised.

This was a startling new concept to young Norman. How anxiously he figured out ways and means to meet his expenses. Could he afford to stop contriving and simply look to God to supply? Would God meet his needs as He had met Muller's? Faith was stirred. In a few month's time, it was to be strongly tested.

Muller's attitude to giving presented Norman with

another tremendous challenge. While never requesting funds from anyone, Muller nevertheless taught as a principle that Christians should give "*voluntary offerings*, whether of money or other means of support, as the proper acknowledgement of service rendered by God's minister, and as a sacrifice acceptable, well-pleasing to God."

This principle strongly influenced Norman's thinking. When preaching on the subject in later years, he would urge, "Give where you have been fed. Your first responsibility is to support those men or organizations through which you yourself have received spiritual benefit."

Out of personal gratitude to God for the contribution of such organizations as Scripture Union and the New Zealand Bible College to his own life and those of his children and grandchildren, Norman has through the years given to them regularly. From a lifetime of giving and receiving he testifies, "Make no mistake, you do indeed reap what you sow!"

Finally, Muller was adamant about the importance of tithing. He believed that, voluntary offerings aside, it is a biblical principle to set apart one-tenth of all income for the work of the Lord. Faithfully he tithed every donation he received for the orphanages and, through the years, was instrumental in passing on huge sums of money to missionary endeavours around the world.

If it's good for George Muller, responded the young reader, *it's good enough for Norman McIntosh!*

He had just received his weekly pay — 7/6. It might as well have been spent already! But carefully he counted out one-tenth — ninepence. Then, because his needs were always greater than his income, he was afraid to keep this money in the hut. If it was too handy, the temptation to use it for other purposes might prove too strong to resist.

So he kept his weekly tithe in a matchbox on a beam of the cowshed roof, quarter of a mile from his hut. He hoped that would be far enough away to cool any attempt to rob the Lord.

Following on from this early temptation has been the

recurring one to "borrow" from the Lord's money and to "bend" the rules so as to supply personal needs or contribute to personal advantage. For anyone in Christian ministry, such manipulation can often be "justified" on the grounds that ultimately it is all for the Lord's work. Norman has always been meticulously careful about this. He takes the Lord's words on the matter very seriously.

"Bring the whole tithe into the storehouse . . . Test me in this," says the Lord Almighty, "and see if I will not throw open the floodgates of heaven and pour out so much blessing that you will not have room enough for it" (Malachi 3:10).

It was a momentous day when this young disciple sent away his first offering from the matchbox. He went in to the Geraldine Post Office, purchased a money order for 2/6 and forwarded it to the Egypt General Mission office in Auckland. This sum probably did not significantly affect the balance sheet of the mission, but it meant everything in his own life, for it was his first financial dealing with God. It launched him into a life of systematic, proportional giving which has been the channel of untold personal blessing and enrichment. It has meant also that, through these gifts, he has had a share in spreading the gospel to many parts of the world where he has never been.

Shortly after he commenced tithing, he purchased a notebook to record all monies received and given from the Lord's account. He has continued this practice throughout his life, and is amazed as he leafs back through the pages to realize what large sums of money he, a poor man, has been able to forward to the Master's work.

From conviction and experience, therefore, he has always challenged believers to give in this way. "You can't be right with God spiritually," he maintains, "if you are not right with Him financially. The Lord's percentage must come first."

At this time Norman had no Christian contact except Bob Morrison. Accordingly, he cycled in to Geraldine twice a week to attend Bible studies in the Morrison home. It was a long haul, but Norman loved the Christian fellowship and soaked up the teaching. Separation from the world was stressed, and he zealously cut himself adrift from all activities he felt were inconsistent with his new-found faith, such as dancing, bridge and horse racing. Eagerly he shared the good news with everyone around him. Then, remembering where he had first heard the gospel, he also commenced a Sunday School in the village school building. The verdict of the community was that Norman McIntosh had religious mania!

While certainly not mad, he was very lonely, with a loneliness that stemmed not so much from a further restricted social life as from being "different." He longed for the companionship of Christian peers but there were few believers in the area.

At a social gathering in another district, he met the local school teacher. She was a keen Christian, a Baptist girl from Ashburton, whose brother was a missionary in China. She had heard of Norman's stand for the Lord and gave him encouragement and some Scripture Union Bible Reading Notes. She also passed on a magazine for his interest. It was *The Baptist.*

Norman has no memory of what that magazine contained except that the inside cover carried an advertisement for the Bible Training Institute of New Zealand . . . "a place where young men and women receive training for missionary service." Interested readers were invited to write to the secretary for further information. Immediately he knew that this was for him. He wrote away and said he wanted to enrol.

The secretary replied promptly and decisively, "You are such a young Christian and you don't even belong to a church yet. We suggest you wait two years and then reapply." It was signed, J Oswald Sanders.

"I cannot wait," Norman wrote back at once, "the matter is urgent!" He tried to explain that the call of the Lord was burning in his heart and he could not delay even two years. As soon as Norman dropped his letter into the postbox, the wait began. *Will they accept me?* he worried over and over again. The rural delivery car came through the valley daily, leaving mail in a box out on the main road a quarter of a mile away. It was Norman's job to ride down and collect it. Every day he approached the box with his heart in his mouth, hoping for, yet dreading the arrival of "the letter." The weeks passed like years before it finally arrived.

He tore open the envelope with trembling fingers and read, "You have been accepted for the BTI course starting February, 1934 . . ." His eyes misted. Accepted! "Thank you, Lord!" he breathed. The letter went on to give instructions for travel and what to do on arrival. It was couched in the most warm and welcoming terms. Norman was overjoyed.

Then he got an awful jolt. "Student fees are 100 pounds per year," the letter concluded. "New students are expected to have the first term's fees in hand when they come in." His heart sank! They might as well have asked for the moon. There was no way on earth that he could ever save anything on 7/6 a week. He felt utterly alone.

"Lord," he cried out despairingly, "You have called me to this place. Somehow I am sure of this. What shall I do now? How shall I get there?"

Now, for the first time, Norman experienced the loving provision of a faithful God. Shortly afterwards, he was led into contact with a friendly sheep shearer whose recommendation gained him a place in a shearing gang as general roustabout and shed hand. This delivered him from the hard and unrewarding grind of his shepherding job and enabled him, in the space of only three months, to save the princely sum of 25 pounds. So with his acceptance by the BTI came the opportunity to earn the required fees.

The financial hurdle was not the only obstacle thrown in his way, however. His family thought he had gone crazy and there seemed to be no way Norman could make them understand what he was doing.

Geraldine, in the South Island of New Zealand, is eight hundred miles by land and sea from Auckland, and few local people had ever heard of the Bible Training Institute (BTI). When the news leaked out that he was going to an institution, it was rumoured around the district that mad Mac was going away for treatment!

But far worse than the opposition of his family and the misunderstanding of the neighbourhood was Mr Morrison's reaction to the news. As a member of the Exclusive Brethren, he viewed an interdenominational college such as the BTI as "a world system" and not for a separated child of God. In any case, formal Bible training of that sort was considered quite unnecessary. This unexpected disapproval from his spiritual father whom he so loved and respected, was a tremendous blow, and just when he thought he'd left all unhappiness behind too!

Norman felt discouraged, confused and isolated. Was he doing the right thing? He could hardly have analyzed what he wanted, but his heavenly Father knew that his greatest need at this time was for the fellowship and support of a church.

Through the Christian school teacher who had given him *The Baptist* magazine, he was invited to attend a Baptist Bible Class Camp from the Ashburton church, 31 miles away. All the campers were strangers but, for him, the whole experience was altogether new and wonderful. On the way back from camp, he was baptized at the Ashburton church and became a member, though an absent one. The love of those folk was very real, however, and through BTI and his subsequent ministry, they backed him warmly as a member of their congregation.

It says a great deal for the large-heartedness of that Christlike man Bob Morrison that, though his spiritual child went to BTI against his convictions and advice and left the Brethren fellowship in which he had been nurtured to join another church, he did not cut him off. On the contrary, he and his son Jack continued with great generosity of spirit to support and encourage Norman all his life. In fact, many years later, Jack and his wife Lois were to render a most beautiful and sacrificial service of love to Norman and his family.

In February 1934, young Norman McIntosh, timid and

quite without normal Christian background and experience, set out for Auckland. In spite of his insecurity, he was conscious of an overflowing sense of privilege that he, a mere farm hand, should be on his way to Bible college.

Many BTI students attended the Baptist Tabernacle which adjoined the BTI premises. But Norman, fresh from the country, felt completely lost in the large, central church. His nervous fear of the sophistication of city folks drove him to find a small congregation in a distant suburb. Grange Road Baptist Church was struggling and rundown. It had no pastor.

Because he was a BTI student, Norman was grabbed for everything — Bible Class leader, Sunday School teacher and leader of the Christian Endeavour. His ignorance of church organization was almost total. He had no idea what Christian Endeavour was, and the first meeting he attended was, of all things, the Annual General Meeting. As leader it was his job to chair this meeting. Diffidently he asked for an explanation of what was required of a chairman.

"It's not difficult," he was informed. "You just have to call for nominations for each appointment, then secure seconders. After that you carry out the vote."

Norman thought he could manage that. He made short work of the meeting — nominating, seconding and voting . . . all by himself! As everyone sat in open-mouthed astonishment at this performance, the Rev. Knowles Kempton, an elderly retired minister, applauded loudly, slapping his knees delightedly and rocking with laughter. It was a never-to-be-forgotten Annual General Meeting. Norman slunk back to BTI that night wondering how he could ever face those people again.

It didn't take the teenage girls in his Bible Class long either to discover that Mr McIntosh was incredibly ignorant, and they teased him unmercifully. On one occasion, when he had finished his lesson early, he asked, "Shall we read a psalm?"

"Oh yes," they replied enthusiastically, "Let's read Psalm

119."

Pleased with this unusual cooperation, he started to read. He had no idea that he'd launched into the longest psalm in the Bible and couldn't figure out what the miserable girls were giggling about — until he turned the page!

The people of this church, however, took this green lad to their hearts, taught him much and generously provided many of his material needs then and later.

At the BTI, he felt himself to be the rawest, shyest and most unpromising student of his year. To earn a little extra money, he accepted the job of Institute scavenger and garbage collector. At the end of his course, the directors wiped off any debts owing in his board account because he had made himself so practically useful about the place. Through this and in a hundred ways, he proved God's faithfulness to supply his every need.

At the BTI he received a thorough grounding in the Scriptures and in practical ministry, but was a very average student, lacking in adequate study skills. Being something of a dreamer, he responded ardently to poetry, art and music but found it difficult to think methodically, outline points logically and make clear applications. An added difficulty was that, having lived all his life on farm and sheep station, he chafed continually at the confines of four walls.

Not surprisingly, the class he dreaded most was homiletics with its staged preaching sessions when the student preacher had to endure class criticism. On one occasion, after Norman's so-called sermon had been reduced to nothing, Mr Sanders tried to save him from complete annihilation by saying, "Mr McIntosh's strong point is earnestness. This quality will often help him through."

In this he spoke a true, prophetic word. Shy and awkward Norman may have been, but there was about him a sincerity and unselfishness which attracted others. People trusted him. They also loved him.

He had a great sense of fun and loved to joke and tease. If there was a prank afoot, he would be sure to be in the middle of it. Like many shy people, he was able to let himself go on such occasions, and his unselfconscious clowning was always a great hit. Privately, though, he had to check his motives. *Am I showing off just to be noticed by others?* This love for "the praise of men" is something he has always consciously resisted.

While in Auckland, he was greatly helped by Dr John Laird of the Scripture Union (SU) and Children's Special Service Mission, who invited him to work among children on the beaches and in camps.

With children Norman could relax and just be himself. They didn't judge his sermons or compare! Wholeheartedly he gave himself to them and they responded with their friendship. Enthusiastic shoals of youngsters, with Norman in their midst, would set out on hikes, play games and build sand castles. He was delighted when he found that his sand pulpit talks got through to them and he was able to lead many to Christ.

Norman had come to BTI with a firm but unspecific call to missionary service. He therefore conscientiously followed up interest in various missions and several countries, seeking the Lord's guidance. For a while India claimed his attention, but this was gradually superseded by a growing burden for the lost millions of China.

A book came into his hands called *Rusty Hinges*, by F D Learner, published by the China Inland Mission. Fascinated, he read of the Tibetans of northwest China, a people totally without Christ. Here was a great unmet need. The reluctant opening of Tibet to the gospel was like a gate swinging on rusty hinges. Norman's heart went out to these people of the grasslands who, like himself, were shepherds and herdsmen. A strong conviction was born in his heart that these people were to be his people and this mission, his mission.

In spite of all his forebodings, he managed to graduate with quite a reasonable pass and earned the prize for "The student who showed the greatest improvement during the session 1934-1935." It was a leatherbound, india paper copy of *Young's Analytical Concordance to the Holy Bible*. That was fifty years ago. Amazingly, it is the one book which, has somehow survived Japanese bombs and Communist confiscation, tropical mould and white ants, and is still in use today.

In every way Norman found BTI a rich, happy and fulfilling experience. Life friendships were formed, and among students and staff he found those whose example he set out to emulate.

One of these was Les Rushbrook, a fellow student, who afterwards became secretary of the BTI. Between them developed one of those rare and beautiful David and Jonathan friendships which, half a century later, is still strong and vital. At that time a Dr Rushbrook was president of the Baptist World Alliance, so Norman nicknamed his friend "Doc." In turn Norman became "Mac."

Of the many people who impressed Norman during his BTI days, none was more significant than a certain senior student named Amy Carter. By the time he was into his second year, she had graduated and was an accepted candidate of the China Inland Mission (CIM).

CHAPTER 3

A ZEALOT FINDS JOY

Amy glanced around the auditorium. Hundreds of friends and well-wishers had gathered to farewell the little band of new missionaries who were about to leave for China. She was one of the band and her heart welled up with gladness because God had chosen her to be His ambassador. There was sadness too as she anticipated parting from so much that was dear and familiar. Somehow, she felt, the whole of her life had been moving towards this end, or rather, this beginning. Her missionary "call" was the call of a lifetime.

Just before she was summoned to the platform, her mother leaned over and whispered, "I want you to know your father dedicated you to be a missionary when you were a baby!"

When Amy was seven years old her father, Henry Carter, had died. Amy and her younger sister Myrle stood beside his open grave ready to drop bunches of violets on to the casket as it was lowered into the ground. Their secure little world had crumbled around them and they were shocked and confused.

Their mother, Ethel, not yet thirty years of age, was all but devastated. She was still mourning the loss of twin babies and a nine-month-old daughter. But she had a staunch faith in God and knew how to draw upon that divine strength which God has promised will be sufficient to meet every human need. Courageously she sold up the home and prepared to start life afresh with her two small daughters.

While she searched for work, the family stayed temporarily with friends.

Because of their recent bereavement, questions of life and death had focused sharply for Amy. Would she ever see her father again? She had also been taught about the Second Coming and was afraid, especially after she'd misbehaved! What if Christ should return and take all the good people away with Him and leave her behind? What if her mother was taken? The thought terrified her.

Night after night, the anxious child would creep along the passage to stand in the eerie darkness outside her mother's door. Was she still there? Amy would listen fearfully until reassured by the sound of regular breathing and then slip back to bed. Somehow her mother discovered what was going on. One night, she drew her little seven year old to her knee and, in the stillness of the candlelit room, explained that when Jesus lives in a person's heart, fears are overcome. "But," she stressed, "He can only live in a clean heart. He will cleanse anyone who comes to Him and says she is truly sorry for her sins."

Moved by God's Spirit, the child responded and by faith asked Jesus into her life. The transaction was recorded, and a piece of yellowed paper bears witness in childish writing to the fact.

Soon after this, both mother and daughter fell victim to the terrible flu epidemic which followed World War I. Many people died. Amy and her mother were not expected to recover, but God spared their lives. They went to the Coromandel Peninsula with grandfather to convalesce, and lived in the open air, cutting cocksfoot and paspalam grasses and beating out the seeds. The sale of these brought in a few needed shillings.

A new life started when the family moved to Napier where the young widow, an expert dressmaker, had the offer of a job. There the girls went to school and life became more normal. Ethel actively pursued the spiritual education of her daughters. She taught them to find their way about the Bible and set them to memorizing Scripture. This was done in such an inspiring way that the girls found it a challenge and enjoyed it with all the thrill of discovery.

Concerned to rear her children faithfully, Ethel maintained strict discipline. Amy, unlike her more docile sister, was a strong-willed, independent child who needed constant correction. This often resulted in resentment and a feeling of "not measuring up." She didn't doubt her mother's love for her, but always yearned for more demonstrative expressions of affection. Many Victorian hymns featured mothers and Amy would often weep with her own longing when such hymns were sung. As she grew older, the protective layer she inevitably built up around herself got thicker and she was able to cover the sore spot with a light laugh.

It was an emotional handicap which she carried into life. In turn, she found it difficult to express her own feelings and would instinctively try to diffuse an emotionally-charged situation by making a bright and breezy comment. This was often unhelpful as people, feeling rebuffed, would go away with the impression that she didn't care. They never realized how deeply she did feel nor saw the tears she shed in private.

When Amy was ten or eleven, a certain business firm ran a colouring competition for children. Eagerly, Amy entered, and did a very thorough job on her copy. But on the day it was to be handed in, she was sick in bed with a cold. She asked a classmate who lived nearby to hand in her precious picture for her. It never reached its destination and Amy was shattered! To think a classmate would do such a thing! The seeds of distrust were sown. She became suspicious of people's motives.

Several incidents of betrayed confidences in subsequent years confirmed this negative attitude. *It would be a nice world*, Amy decided, *if there were no people!* With Christian maturity this reaction modified but she always had to fight an instinctive tendency to suspect or withdraw from people with whom she had no special affinity. At the end of a lifetime she declares, "My deepest gratitude goes to those trustworthy friends whose uncritical love has been my greatest encouragement to trust myself more openly to others."

Missionaries and missionary literature early had a place in Amy's life. Miss Nellie MacDuff, a family friend, was prayed for every night. Her letters from China were eagerly read by them all.

So it was not surprising that Amy, at age eleven and full of zeal for the missionary cause, decided to do something to help Miss MacDuff. She was, by that time, developing a fair skill at sewing and knitting and, under her mother's tutelage, had already started making her own clothes. On this occasion, she bought a small doll for a shilling, dressed it attractively, and then sold it for twice the amount. A trading project began which soon drew the interest and involvement of a number of friends.

One Saturday, they held a small sale of things made or contributed. The grand sum of 12 pounds was realized. A generous adult subsidized this amount and 24 pounds was forwarded to Miss MacDuff through the China Inland Mission.

Away in Honan Province, a little group of Christians prayed for a place where they could meet for worship. A building was available and, because it was rumoured to be haunted, it was going cheap. The believers knew that Christ was stronger than any evil spirit, and they were willing to buy.

But with what? Just at this juncture came the gift from New Zealand. The purchase was made and the title deeds bear the name, "The Amy and Myrle Carter Gospel Hall."

Two delighted little girls in New Zealand felt they had a personal stake in that faraway land. For Amy it was an important link in the chain of guidance by which she was directed to China. Myrle later married Stan Conway, the son of Honan missionaries, and the couple have been lifelong supporters of the CIM.

The years in Napier were noteworthy because of two other pieces that were to be fitted into God's pattern for their lives.

While still at primary school, Amy and Myrle were among many children invited to hear a British speaker from the Children's Special Service Mission, an organization not yet established in New Zealand. He held his meetings in the open-air beside the paddling pool on Napier's beautiful Marine Parade. Gathered in the sunshine, scores of children heard a happy, vital message. Amy was thrilled, and little dreamed that it was the beginning of a long association with the movement.

Also at Napier, Ethel and her children attended the little Baptist Church where the Rev. M.W.P. Lascelles was minister. After years as a successful businessman, he had become a pastor, and was a very mature friend and counsellor to many who heard the gospel through him.

During World War I, he had been a YMCA Commissioner on a troopship that was torpedoed in the Mediterranean. As he floated in the sea, the Bible in his pocket, which had been heavily underlined in red, got soaked. The ink ran through the pages and the "pink" Bible ever after held tremendous fascination for Amy.

During their years in the church, a warm friendship grew between the Carters and the pastor who was a widower. When he was asked to become Secretary of the Baptist Union and Treasurer of the Baptist Missionary Society, it meant a shift to Wellington. He did not go alone. Friendship had blossomed into something deeper and, before taking up his new post, he married Ethel. So God gave Amy and Myrle a wise and caring father whom they loved and respected.

From the time she was a little girl, Amy loved to write, both poetry and prose, and won several writing competitions. Also she was fascinated by living and growing things. She made a special study of New Zealand flora and built up a large collection of pressed specimens. Wherever she went in later years, her observant study of the native flora added a rich interest to life.

Amy trained as a primary school teacher, with special qualifications in music. She was a gifted pianist and singer and every week, with several others, broadcast to schools over the national network. Through this and her teaching practice, she also gained poise and became a capable public speaker.

In the local church, her musical ability was put to good use. As organist, choir member and conductor of a children's choir, she was often in the limelight. Not surprisingly, another would-be musician, motivated by jealousy, caused her a great deal of hurt. This sort of thing was no isolated incident. Amy's all-round ability often provoked jealousy in others and she couldn't handle it. Deeply wounded, she determined, *If people don't like me, I'll just keep away from them!*

It wasn't until later she began to realize that, while some jealousy was inevitable, she *could* do more to build others up. Just after she started at Bible Training Institute, Mrs Sanders pointed out to her that other people who didn't play the piano as well as she would also be asked to play.

"While I," laughed Amy, "sit back and gnash my teeth!" She never forgot Mrs Sander's reply.

"It'll be a sign of grace when you don't gnash your teeth!"

Amy was single-minded in her dedication to the Lord, and threw herself wholeheartedly into His service. For five years she taught Sunday School and zealously took on all manner of tasks in the church. But underneath all her busyness was a growing dissatisfaction with life in general. What was wrong?

It was the custom for her parents, after the family had gone to bed, to kneel beside the dying embers of the fire and pray together.

One night after Amy had retired, she remembered there was a telephone call to make. The phone was just outside the living room door. During a pause, she heard a voice in prayer asking that "Amy might have more joy in her service for the Lord." She was appalled. Didn't her parents know how much she was doing for the Lord? She went to bed in high dudgeon.

But God heard that prayer.

At nineteen years of age, Amy was invited to spend a

holiday with friends in another city. They took her to their church and the minister there showed her what was wrong, very wrong in her life. For the first time she was made aware that the Holy Spirit is a Person, indeed God Himself — God, the Holy Spirit, and third Person of the Trinity. The pastor spoke on "Resist not, grieve not, quench not the Spirit of God." Amy was deeply stirred and convicted.

In the evening, the preacher again pointed out, "There must be a full surrender of a person's will to Christ before the Holy Spirit can work in that person and through him or her in blessing to others." He asked all young people 28 years and under to stay behind for another meeting. There, he requested everyone who was willing to say "Yes" to the Lord Jesus to make a public commitment.

The struggle was on! To promise to agree to anything God would appoint for her life? To let the decision be His, *whatever* it might be?

There was no escaping the issue. It had to be total abdication of self. God's will for hers. Nothing less would do. There could be no compromise if there was to be spiritual progress.

"Yes Lord," she whispered as she stood up, "Your will, not mine, in everything!"

Amy went to bed that night emotionally exhausted but at peace with God. Next morning she woke up to a new world. The sky seemed brilliantly blue and an unspeakable joy filled heart and mind as she tried to describe events to her hostess. The Spirit of God was in control. She was transformed. On the first Sunday back in Wellington, she was once more with her class of eleven-year-old girls. Something new happened.

In the previous five years, she had not seen one child come to Christ. Her aim had been to prepare and teach a lesson well, with no realization that the first responsibility is to lead children to Christ.

And now? Five girls stayed behind after class, and wanted to ask the Lord Jesus to come into their hearts. Years later, one of these girls said to her, "If you could have seen your face that Sunday after your holiday! We all wanted what you'd got!"

The Scriptures came alive to her in a personal way and prayer became a reality. There was a new concern for others and joy bubbled up in her soul. It was her third year at Teachers' College. Immediately she collected five other Christian women students. Together they found a secluded spot under a tree and, in their lunch hours, interceded for others. The Lord met them and there was thrill and strength as they prayed. Not surprisingly, four of the six went as missionaries to countries around the world.

The fruits of the Spirit became more evident in Amy's behaviour. She was immensely cheered one day when her mother and Myrle expressed amazement at her unusual patience over a certain matter. She realized with gratitude that God was at work in her life in every way.

During this year, her interest in China deepened into a clear personal directive. But there was one serious barrier. Her father had died of pulmonary tuberculosis. The China Inland Mission had recently turned down applications from two of her good friends because of a family medical history. The conflict became almost unbearable between the urge to offer to the CIM and this impossible situation. The climax came after six months.

As she sat behind the organ playing for an evening Communion service, she cried in her heart, "Lord, show me from your Word whether it is China or not." A verse from the Old Testament and one from the New combined to give His answer. "Go unto this people . . . for I have chosen thee." She never doubted His voice. Later she was examined by a leading TB specialist who found her in perfect health and told the CIM he didn't believe in hereditary tuberculosis.

The following year she entered the Bible Training Institute.

During her first year there, she had the joy of pointing 42 people to Christ and seeing them make a commitment. In the second year, one hundred people did the same. The Holy

Spirit was moving in Auckland in those days, perhaps because of all the prayer that was going up for the W P Nicholson missions. Amy's "chance" encounters with people in unlikely places led to many immediate conversions. Everywhere she found prepared hearts.

She used to go out "fishing" in her lunch breaks. Once at a bus stop she chatted with a worried-looking woman who told her how she'd been having nightmares about falling into hell. As the bus approached, Amy quickly outlined God's way of salvation, pushed her own New Testament into the lady's hand and told her where to read.

"If you want to talk further," she called as the woman clambered aboard the bus, "I'll meet you next Monday on that seat over there." The woman was there and Amy led her to the Saviour.

Another day, Amy was attracted to an elderly lady who stood staring unseeingly into a shop window. She was gowned in heavy, black mourning and her face was desolate. As Amy got talking with her, she broke down.

"Look at these," she wept, pulling out a locket on a chain around her neck. On either side was the picture of a young man, her sons. "This one, the younger, has just died."

"You had *two* sons, and one has died," said Amy gently. "God had *one* Son and He gave Him to die for you." With growing eagerness, this grieving woman drank in the words of salvation and there, on the busy Queen Street footpath, she professed her faith in Christ.

This fruitfulness was a great joy to Amy. It was wonderful confirmation that God would use her as His missionary.

Towards the end of her course, the Lord spoke to her through His Word one morning. "Gather up the fragments that remain, that nothing be lost" (John 6:12). She knew He meant her to track down those who had made a commitment and to do a bit of follow-up before she left Auckland. It was quite marvellous how God helped her to contact so many.

For instance, one of the "fragments" was the lady of the bus stop. Amy had lost trace of her for fifteen months.

Towards the end of her BTI course, Amy was assisting at a down-town mission. Who should walk in one Sunday night but this very woman and her husband! She was a radiant Christian. Only the Lord could have brought this to pass. Such experiences strengthened Amy's faith and she took God's Word literally.

Too literally, perhaps, for when a leading Christian preacher was on his death bed, she announced confidently that the Lord had shown her he was going to get better. He died! Ever after that she shied away from any dogmatic claim that "The Lord told me!" particularly in relation to other people.

With her intense desire to be all out for God, Amy, in her youth, saw life as divided into "spiritual" and "secular," and avoided those activities she considered of little spiritual worth. Soon after arrival in China, she was asked to speak at a teachers' college on "New Zealand," but refused to do so because she couldn't see it as a spiritual opportunity. As she grew in grace and the knowledge of God and His ways, she learned to rub out the line between spiritual and secular. Washing the dishes, she came to realize, could be just as sacred an activity as preaching the gospel, if done in the right attitude.

Amy had left BTI with her sights set on China. Although she had a number of admirers, she had responded to none of them, believing that it was the highest possible calling for her to go to the mission field single. Her heroines were such outstanding women as Amy Carmichael and Mary Slessor. It had never entered her mind that Norman McIntosh was looking her way or that it could possibly be in God's will for their paths to merge.

CHAPTER 4

TO CHINA WITH LOVE

In those days at BTI, the sexes were strictly segregated. So when Norman fell in love, there was not much he could do about it. *In any case*, he told himself, *it's quite useless for someone like me to aspire to the hand of a girl like Amy Carter*. Despair gave rise to another friendship, but the Lord prevented his making any serious mistake.

Try as he would, he could not get Amy out of his mind and heart, so he took the matter to God in prayer for nearly two years. By then Amy had left BTI and was preparing to go to China with the CIM. Before his own graduation, Norman knew that God had called him also to serve in China and with the same mission.

In the process of filling out his application papers, he came to a question, "Are you interested in any young lady?" In all honesty, he couldn't write "No," and in decency he couldn't answer "Yes" without consulting the lady.

Now it so happened that Amy had been unable to proceed to China because of unsettled conditions there. No single women were permitted to go forward that year unless they were nurses or were engaged to marry someone already there. This was a keen disappointment at the time, but as Amy was to discover, this delay was no mere accident of circumstances. God had His purpose in it for her.

About the time Norman was filling out his papers, both of them happened to be attending a Children's Special Service Mission house party under the leadership of Dr Laird. Day after day, the nervous young man tried to muster the courage to test his suit.

The surroundings were beautiful and a silver moon shone by night. Could there have been a more romantic time to make a proposal? But the lovely nights were wasted. The great moment came on a public highway about eleven o'clock in the morning with people passing to and fro!

Norman had just blurted out his side of the case when a group of fellows came running up.

"Mac," they puffed urgently, "Come and help! Galloping Gertie (an old car) is stuck in the ditch!" And away they raced with helpful Mac hard at their heels.

He must have come back for his answer and been accepted for, as a happily engaged couple, Norman and Amy sailed ten months later for China.

The intervening time was not without its tests, however. After the house party, Amy was assailed by doubt. It was not her feelings for Norman that were in question but her high-minded resolve to go to the mission field single. Was she being seduced from the will of the Lord by a human love? After a long talk with Dad Lascelles, who wisely advised her just to wait and see, she received an urgent request to play the piano for a women's meeting. Now Amy, who later was to have a nationwide ministry among women, had at that time a decided antipathy to women's work and wasn't too pleased to receive this request.

The meeting was all she expected and she suffered it until the Bible reading. The reader was a funny little woman in a funnier old hat but suddenly, what she was reading hit Amy between the eyes, "If it were not so, I would have told you." Immediately she knew that God had spoken and her troubled heart was filled with peace. From that day on, she had never a doubt that Norman and she were meant for each other.

After graduation, Norman joined the BTI evangelists Jack and Mary Miller on the Kemp Memorial Caravan. They travelled around the country areas of the North Island visiting, witnessing and preaching, and the whole experience was exceptionally good training for a missionary candidate.

Norman assisted the Millers in practical ways. He also led the singing and arranged children's meetings. During one mission, Jack, who was the evangelist, fell ill and Norman had to step in and take his place. Overwhelmed by the challenge, he fell on his face before the Lord, then tremblingly took the platform for the last two nights. At both meetings people were converted!

It never seemed to stop raining in Taranaki, the cow country. At one rough farm house where they were billeted, there were texts on the walls. Leaks had effaced some of the letters, so that "Let not your heart be troubled" became "Le . . ot your heart be troubled." Jack had a wooden leg and an indomitable spirit. Not infrequently at night he would catch his artificial foot in long grass and take a tumble. "Le . . ot, Mac, "le . . ot!" he would bellow and Norman would grope around in the dark to find him and haul him on to his feet. "Le . . ot" became their war cry and courage booster. It echoed on into the years ahead, a challenge to trust God through many a troubled situation.

While Norman was on the Caravan, Amy relieved the travelling secretary of the Girls' Crusader Union for nine months. In this capacity she ranged the length and breadth of New Zealand encouraging secondary school pupils in their witness for Christ and introducing many young people to the CIM and its ministry.

During those months, the couple scarcely saw one another. Was God, even then, preparing them for the many separations that would lie ahead?

Thrifty Mac was delighted when a kindly old stationer gave him a stack of notepaper samples left by various commercial travellers. Every sheet was different and each had a clipped corner. On this paper Norman wrote to his fiancee. Amy was not so pleased. She, a lover of the neat and attractive, felt she deserved better than this! Years later she used to laugh about her idealistic fussiness and say, "I'm glad to get anything now, even written on the back of a bus ticket!"

She never had any complaint about the contents of these missives, however. Norman wrote beautiful letters full of his devotion to her and to the Lord.

Eventually their departure date was set. The valedictory meeting came and went and final goodbyes were said. At last they were off to China. Norman, lacking the understanding support of a Christian family, loved Amy's mother as his own. Throughout the years of their missionary career this woman of prayer was the central focus of their support, emotionally and spiritually. They gave her their complete confidence and she prayed them through many a personal crisis.

In those days of sea travel to the Far East, CIM parties were required to go first to Australia and then on by boat to China. Special permission was granted for Norman and Amy to travel together on the *S S Wanganella* as far as Sydney. But after that each was to go separately to Shanghai escorted by senior missionaries! Marriage had to be deferred until certain language requirements were met, usually two years after arrival in China.

Amy sailed from Australia on the *S S Nellore* with four other young women and their escorts, arriving in Shanghai on 8 October 1936. Norman left on the *S S Changte* and arrived four days later. He was the only male recruit from "Down Under" that year and, as he set off on his solitary voyage from Sydney, the Lord lovingly arranged a special farewell for him which gladdened his heart. Of all people, Bob and Jack Morrison had been in Australia on a business trip and they stood on the wharf waving until the ship disappeared from sight.

Norman's passage had been prepaid to China by the CIM, but just before his departure from Auckland, Mr H S Conway, the New Zealand Secretary, asked, "Do you have sufficient money for expenses en route?" Feeling that this was a test of faith, Norman assured him that he had — seven pounds eleven shillings! What he hadn't realized was that in Australia, while waiting for the China ship, he would need to pay board. So when he sailed from Sydney, he had only a few coppers left in his pocket. Burning with embarrassment, he had to tip the table steward with some unused Australian postage stamps, and disembarked in China without a penny in the world!

As their vessels steamed up the river into Shanghai and passed by the bows of warships from China, Great Britain, USA, France and Japan, these young people from safe, faraway New Zealand felt for the first time the chilly breeze of international tension. Anti-foreign feeling was running high in China in those days, and many times Norman and Amy were to be startled by the hatred they saw in the eyes of people who passed them on the street.

Norman had been afraid he would miss Amy at Shanghai. As the *Changte* drew in to dock, he anxiously scanned the crowd of people milling about the wharf. Hundreds of coolies were waiting to swarm aboard. His heart lurched! There she was, waving, and looking more beautiful than ever in these strange surroundings.

He couldn't get off the ship quickly enough and remembered only just in time that he'd been warned, "No embraces in public!" Such open displays of affection were offensive to the Chinese. Even holding hands was taboo. After this long month of separation, it was great to be able to enjoy a few precious days together at the CIM headquarters before proceeding inland to their respective language schools.

They found it terribly hard to say goodbye again, knowing they would see so little of each other in the next two years. "We feel we can't wait so long," they prayed. "Lord, help us to do Your will wholeheartedly and cheerfully."

As they travelled up the Yangtze River, they soaked in the sights and sounds of the new land. The paddy fields, dry and brown at this season, would be brilliant green and beautiful in the spring. Then the newcomers would be revolted to discover that these fields were little better than cesspools. Nothing was wasted in old China and the crops were fertilized with human manure. They were appalled by the squalor and poverty in which so many of the people lived. Their hearts went out to the swarms of children with their mischievous black eyes and grubby faces. These youngsters wore permanent splits in their trousers, which the new missionaries quickly dubbed "the wide open spaces." Little bottoms, blue with cold, became a common sight.

By this time Norman and Amy too had donned the traditional blue and black Chinese clothing and were feeling decidedly bulky in their wadded winter gowns. Strange it all was, but they were glad to be there and longed to be able to reach out to the needy people of this vast country.

Norman travelled to the men's language school in the company of a bright young couple from another country, also new missionaries. They were both university graduates, knowledgeable, confident, aggressive, and Norman's self-esteem had sunk to a record low by the time they reached their destination. What on earth did he have to bring to the people of China alongside these shining lights?

His progress at language school was quite satisfactory, despite the setback of a severe case of measles. Later, he became proficient at writing Chinese characters with a brush, a skill not mastered by many, but was always rather hampered in the spoken language by being tone deaf. Altogether he found language study a hard grind. Inevitably, as he sized himself up against men from North America, Britain and the Continent who were well-educated, gifted and socially poised, he would feel besieged by self-doubt.

He remembered what Mr Gardiner, CIM representative in Sydney, had said as they were driving in the taxi to the wharf. "We recognize and value the variety of gifts in new workers. Some are thinkers and students, others are 'doers.' Both will contribute in their own way."

I can never aspire to being more than a doer, was Norman's silent reaction. In his insecurity, his greatest fear was that he might be a failure. Again and again he cried, "O use me, Lord, use even me."

With growing experience and maturity, he was later able

to see himself and others more objectively, but has never been able to throw off this inferiority complex completely. While he was always to feel woefully inadequate for each new challenge, he never evaded doing what he knew to be God's will, and it was this very lack of self-confidence that kept him dependent upon the Lord and humble in his attitude to others.

He worried a good deal about the political situation. The influence of the Japanese in the north and the Communists in the northwest was making it increasingly difficult for missionaries to enter the area. In his heart Norman had a deep longing to go to Tibet in the far northwest, but hadn't the courage to voice this preposterous idea to the director who advised him about his designation.

If this desire is from God, Norman believed, *I must trust Him to open the way, and not try to push things through myself.*

After six months at language school, he was sent to work with a young Australian bachelor, Bob Ament, in a mountain station in South Shaanxi. He was glad that, at least, he was heading in the right direction. Shaanxi was in the northwest region.

At the women's language school in Yangzhou, Jiangsu Province, Amy was discovering that there were many things to learn besides language. Coming from a very small country, the New Zealanders found themselves often irked by the "superior" attitude of some who felt they were the CIM, originating as they did from lands where the mission had long been established. In such an international situation, national pride could become amazingly prickly and a source of tension.

It was the custom on Sunday afternoons for each woman in turn to speak about her own country, giving some spiritual overtones. When Amy's turn came, she thought, "I'll show them!" Hanging on the wall was a big map of the world. She swung round to point out her beloved homeland and, lo and behold, it wasn't there! Whoever had prepared that map hadn't even included New Zealand, God's Own Country!

When the laughter had subsided, she struggled on. Somewhere in her talk came the illustration of a small boat on the Mississippi River. Every time it blew its whistle, the engine stopped. There wasn't steam for both! Afterwards a young American came up to Amy and snapped, "Why'd you put that boat on the Mississippi? Why didn't you put it on one of your little New Zealand rivers?"

All newcomers had lessons to learn as they adjusted, not only to China, but to each other. There were 52 women in that group and they came from fourteen countries. By God's grace many strong and loving international friendships were formed and the lives of each enriched accordingly.

With their first language exam successfully behind them, Norman and Amy looked forward to meeting again. The mission leaders considerately arranged for them to have a few days together in Zhenjiang. There they roamed the country-side, seeing among other places the childhood home of Pearl Buck, the novelist who has charmed countless readers with her stories about old China.

Amy was also designated to Shaanxi, to the small town of Fengxian on the border of Gansu Province. Her senior missionary was Miss Ruby Thompson from America who had been in China many years. Mrs Li, a capable Bible woman, set out to befriend the green newcomer and took her trips into the surrounding country area to visit in peasant homes.

One visit left an indelible impression and also acted as a warning. With Mrs Li, Amy entered a tiny mountain shack and found a sad, despondent man sitting on the edge of the kang (mud brick bed). He was blind. When the Bible woman started to talk to him about Jesus, bitterness overflowed.

Apparently, some years before, an over-zealous and immature evangelist from another part of China had visited this man. Enthusiastically, the preacher had assured him that if only he would believe in Christ, his sight would be restored.

"I tried sincerely to believe in Christ," said the man, "but nothing happened. As you see," he added bitterly, "I am still blind." He had lost what faith he had and great damage had been done. He did not want to hear any more, and no amount of gentle talk about a loving Saviour had any effect.

This and similar experiences have made Norman and Amy rather cautious in the area of divine healing, but they have rejoiced when, from time to time, God has wonderfully demonstrated His healing power. For instance, at one time a fellow worker developed a growth on the side of her nose near her eye. It was diagnosed as malignant. In a panic, she sent word to her home church. Three hundred people gathered to pray for her. She never knew when the miracle occurred, but one morning she looked in her mirror and the growth had disappeared completely.

Norman and Amy had not long settled into their new assignments when, on 7 July 1937, the Sino-Japanese War erupted. From then until they finally left China fifteen years later, they were to serve in a country racked by war.

The whole of Shaanxi Province was seething with unrest. Warlords and brigands preyed upon one area after another. During the fifteen months they were together, Bob Ament and Norman acted as stopgaps at various stations during the absence of other missionaries. One afternoon, in the process of trying to reach the sacked station of Zeyang they arrived at a village, only to realize too late that they had walked into the arms of the soldiers of robber chief Wang Tsan Tsuen. The brigands threw them into a small room and locked the door. About two in the morning, while their captors were still gambling and drinking out the front, the young men successfully scraped a hole in the thick mud wall at the back. They crawled through and fell into the muck of a pigsty. Somehow they managed to grope their way out without disturbing the pigs, and didn't stop running till noon!

During these months, Norman gained valuable experience. He and Bob hiked or cycled hundreds of miles to preach the gospel, often on the streets, and to circulate the Scriptures in the villages. At a boys' camp Norman was encouraged to witness six lads come to Christ.

Perhaps one of the greatest trials to bear was the dislocation of the mail service. For weeks on end there would be no overseas mail. On her way through Hong Kong the year before, Amy had been fascinated by the inscription engraved over the entrance to the Post Office. "As cold waters to a thirsty soul, so is good news from a far country!" How true! Separated from one another and with limited language preventing very satisfying communication with the Chinese, they too thirsted for the letters that often never came.

Permission for Norman and Amy to marry was granted early in 1938. As they looked forward to their wedding and subsequent service together, they took a further step of commitment.

Not long after arriving in Shaanxi, Amy had received a note from a revered senior lady missionary. "Dear fellow pilgrim," it urged, "keep your standards high!" She thought she'd heard from an angel, until she discovered this was part of a campaign to enlist her support for a mutiny against the Superintendent. She was shocked and disillusioned. It was not a happy introduction.

Norman too had witnessed the sorry results of clashes between missionaries and their leaders. The newcomers, while naturally idealistic, were sensible enough to realize that conflict situations were bound to occur from time to time. What should their own attitude be?

"As I see it," said Norman, "the Lord has put us into a team. Therefore He is not likely to lead us independently of that team."

"Also," added Amy, "the Bible is quite clear that we should be in submission to those who are over us in the Lord. It isn't unreasonable then to expect God to guide us through our leaders."

They recalled the solemn occasion two years earlier when together they had buried the word "can't". If God's will should come to them via mission directives, how then could they say "can't," or, worse still, "won't?"

"But, Norm, what if a leader really should make a wrong

decision?" queried Amy.

"We pray, and trust God to overrule any mistakes," he replied. "Surely, this is a better way than to take things into our own hands and oppose directives whenever we don't like them."

Amy fervently agreed. "Lord," they covenanted, "as You have called us into the CIM, we will accept any request made of us by our mission leaders as from You. We will trust You to overrule any possible error of judgment."

Neither Norman nor Amy are naturally meek, submissive people who easily bow to authority, neither have they laboured under the delusion that all mission leaders are infallible. Throughout their missionary career, they have often questioned mission policies and practices, but as far as they personally are concerned, they have remained faithful to their commitment to the CIM through fifty years. And God has honoured their stand. If mistakes have occurred, He has brought good out of them for these two who have so fully trusted in Him.

Half a world away from home and loved ones, at Chengdu, Sichuan, Norman and Amy were married. The wedding finery she had prepared for the great day never arrived and was not to be unpacked for eleven years.

There was a scurry to get everything ready. Amy bought a length of cloth locally and ran up a wedding gown on a borrowed hand-machine. Her veil was a long piece of tulle left by a doctor's wife for the use of successive brides.

"And, of course, we will have white flowers," decided Amy, the traditionalist. But the flowers were organized by someone else. After a draughty ride in a windowless "taxi," the bride was met at the church by her acting father, Dr Lechler, and was revolted to see a bright pink camelia in the lapel of his grey suit!

The love of the CIM "family" enfolded the young couple on their wedding day and their hearts were deeply moved as Douglas Sargent spoke from Mark 3:14. "Jesus chose Amy and Norman that they should be with Him and that He might send them forth to preach." The closing hymn expressed their personal pledge for the years ahead, "O Jesus, we have promised to serve you to the end."

Joyfully they set out for the little mountain town of Shiquan in Southeast Shaanxi. What would their first home be like?

It was one in a row of shops, the front opening on to the street. There the preaching chapel had pride of place. The premises were narrow, and at the back were built high on the city wall. This wall stood on a steep cliff which fell far down to the great Han river below.

There was no garden but a small open space where a couple of short lines were hung for the washing. Over the wall, in the next-door yard, pigs were slaughtered for the village butcher, usually at about three in the morning. Sleep was shattered when the victims began to squeal.

Under their small bedroom, Norman built a framed platform on which to keep goats. Sometimes it seemed they spent most of the night stomping about. Once a snake shed its skin nearby, and on another occasion Norman killed a large one. They were not without company!

It was a humble little house, but Amy soon had it comfortable and homelike, and they were very happy. The outreach at Shiquan, although commenced earlier by Miss Rachael Begbie and her companion, was still very much in the pioneer stage. There was no formal church, only a handful of believers. Norman had to assume leadership and responsibility for the ongoing development of the work. This was the first time either of them had been on their own without missionary supervision. It was quite a challenge because when problems cropped up, there was nobody to consult. They just had to act on their own initiative. This brought them to a new reliance upon the Lord and a new realization of the vital necessity of prayer.

Fortunately, there was a national evangelist in the area who was supported by the mission. Norman was glad to be able to go out preaching and tracting with Pastor Tsu, because he was still far from fluent in Chinese himself and would have floundered on his own.

The people were very idolatrous and superstitious in their fear of spirits. No field in the surrounding countryside was without its spirit tokens and offerings. No home was without its idol shelf on which incense sticks smouldered and food was offered to various deities and the ancestor spirits. Satan and his demons held these people captive and they were not very responsive to the gospel.

So it was a great joy when a farmer, who reminded them of a biblical patriarch, brought out his household gods and publicly burned them as he confessed his faith in Christ. The man had two wives. The elder was terrified by what was happening. Amy saw her sneak a small piece of an image and, when nobody was looking, hide it round the side of the stove. How human! For she had nothing as yet to replace this idol in her life.

With this man's conversion, the Christians were faced with the question, "Can a man be received into fellowship when he has two wives?" Should he abandon one? If so, which one? They struggled with this and searched the Scriptures for the answer. In the South Shaanxi churches at that time, no general policies had yet been made in regard to such issues. Finally, the Macs with the believers concluded that the man must not abandon his second wife. It would be unchristian and cruel. He might take Communion but would be disqualified from holding office in the church.

About the time World War II erupted in faraway Europe, a frightful cholera epidemic broke out in their immediate vicinity. It was probably spread by retreating soldiers. These men were a pitiful sight. Often a string of them with diseased eyes, and sometimes blind, trailed through the town, each with a walking stick and clinging to the man in front. At the height of the plague, one hundred and fifty people a day were dying of cholera. School children alert in the morning were dead by afternoon.

In panic the local officials fled, leaving the people to fend for themselves. Eventually, a team of public-spirited university students came from Central China to help inoculate the people. The Christians offered their chapel as an emergency clinic and Norman gave himself all day long to assist the students in their job.

Amy, looking down from the tiny back verandah of their home, was appalled to see dying people crawl into the river in a vain attempt to cool their raging fever. Beside them stood the water-carriers, filling their buckets with water to be used in household water butts!

Although Norman and Amy had been inoculated against cholera, it was hard not to be anxious when, at the height of the epidemic, their first daughter was born. The risks were enormous. They named me Linnet and gave me the Chinese name of Ai-Do (Greatly loved).

One night, while I was still a tiny baby, my parents were unable to sleep because of the ceaseless wailing of another infant. Where was it, and why? Just below the top of the city wall a ledge jutted out on which several untidy, thatched dwellings of the very poor found precarious footing.

In the morning, Norman climbed down there to investigate and found a mother and baby lying in the blazing summer sun. The woman, dying with cholera, had been cast out by her terrified relatives. Norman hurried to make a shade over her, but it was too late to save her life. He attended to the burial and then brought home the baby nobody wanted.

Suddenly there were twin girls in the family, Linnet and "Ruth." She was a poor little scrap. Would they be able to save her? Miraculously she was free from cholera, but was dehydrated and covered with scabies. Norman forbad Amy to touch her until he had first cleaned her up with sulphur and lime. Then, lovingly they tended her, and Ruth soon became fat and rosy. But whatever were they to do with her?

They loved her but could not keep her. It was against mission policy in those days to adopt a national child, so Norman and Amy prayed that the Lord would provide a home for her. In Chinese society, girl babies were not in demand and so it was wonderful when a couple in the church offered to take her. They had one small daughter and said they'd like to have Ruth to make a pair in the home. Amy dressed the little one in a flowery red wadded suit, and she went cheerfully to her new family.

Not only were the mountain peasants bound by fear and a prey to epidemic diseases, but they suffered from malnutrition. Huge goitres, due to diet deficiencies, were common. Sometimes these hung down almost to the waist. Skin and eye diseases were part of living. Deaths were common and Norman and Amy were often sickened by the generally callous attitude towards suffering. Life was held very cheap.

Outlaws constantly terrorized the people. The country was at war and it was not easy for authorities to keep up with everything that happened in small, out-of-the-way places. Thieving was rife and brigand chiefs took full advantage of the situation. One frightening day several men were decapitated and their heads hung in the city street as a warning to evildoers.

Then, all too often, there were natural disasters. When the Han River was in flood, yellow water boiled through the gorge carrying trees, animals and even whole thatched houses. Amy watched, white-faced and impotent, as a man floated by, clinging to a rooftop, shrieking *"Jiu ming! Jiu ming!"*(Save life! Save life!)There was no way to reach him as he swept on towards the rapids.

Norman and Amy were frequently frustrated because there was so little they could do to improve the lot of these poor peasants. Again and again, they had to remind themselves that their commission was to "save life" by pointing people to Christ. Through Him alone could come the power to change all of life.

After about eighteen months, however, their ministry in this mountain village came to a sudden end. The McIntoshes were surprised to be asked to leave Shiquan and take over the central station at Hanzhong. The Superintendent's departure on an extended furlough had created a shortage of personnel at the regional headquarters. Norman was to act as Local Secretary for all the field workers, while Amy was to be hostess of the mission home.

They would go, of course, but faced the new appointment with mixed feelings. It was hard to leave the fledgling church at Shiquan but they were excited by the challenge of wider opportunities in Hanzhong. It was a very responsible post.

Norman was again nagged by the fear of possible failure. Would he be able to cope? He had no business experience and little knowledge of bookkeeping. But "can't" had been buried, so they must hold to God's promise to help them accomplish His will.

I was nine months old when they set off for the new sphere of service. In 1940, the two-storeyed house in Hanzhong was the nerve-centre of missionary activity for the whole area. Workers came in all the time on business or for medical purposes. Norman and Amy felt God prompting them to give themselves in love to the needs of these fellow workers, to care for them in every way possible and to make the home a restful, happy place.

During the two-and-a-half years they held the fort there, over three hundred guests stayed for shorter or longer periods. Sick missionaries needed nursing or to have special diets prepared for them, a baby was born and the beloved Acting Superintendent passed away with typhoid fever after a month's illness.

As an added service, Norman set up a kind of business department. Many staple commodities were becoming scarce. Whenever he could, he would buy in bulk such items as soap, candles and medicine, and so supply the needs of outlying stations.

Through it all, Japanese bombers carried out incessant air raids. At first, everyone just ran into the fields to hide in the wheat. Moonlight nights were especially feared, and often Norman and Amy went to bed fully dressed. When the alert sounded, they sprang up, grabbed me out of my cot, and hurried by rickshaw or on foot with the escaping throng. There was real danger of being trampled to death as frightened people stampeded through the city gates away from likely bombing targets.

In the mercy of God, the mission house was spared, though the Macs often went back to sweep up fallen plaster. As the house next door was occupied by the number one military general, and was also near the airfield, their deliverance was all the more remarkable.

Soon the constant running began to wear them out. Finally, Norman decided the time had come to construct a dugout in the garden. Because the water table was high, it was not possible to dig very deep, but he was able to build a small refuge with mounds of earth piled on top. Many times in the days ahead, the Macs and their guests had to run to the dugout for shelter.

Once when a number of missionaries were gathered for a day of prayer, the first air alert sounded at nine in the morning. Planes soon appeared, not once, but in five waves, hour after hour. No "all clear" could be given, so they stayed in the cramped quarters of the dugout, singing for the sake of the children, to deaden the sound of falling bombs.

When it was finally over, something after midday, they crawled with trembling knees up the few steps into the sunshine where they lay to thaw out for a while! Presently, round the corner of the house came the cook boy. With all the sang-froid in the world he asked, "Will you have dinner served here or inside?"

It was so unexpected that everyone burst out laughing and tension was relieved. The lad told them that, throughout the raid, he had just gone on preparing the meal. Every time the bombs started to fall, he ducked under the cooking bench! The children raced around the garden picking up lots of bright, new brass toys — empty cartridge cases from the strafing planes.

Because of the increasing attention Hanzhong was receiving from enemy planes, fellow missionaries decided that Amy, who was heavily pregnant, should take me and go a mile or two into the countryside at night to sleep in a small farmhouse. This she did the first night, and found next morning that we had reposed peacefully alongside an ammunition dump!

On the anniversary of the outbreak of the Sino-Japanese War, the second McIntosh daughter was born. Averil was also given a Chinese name, Ai-Hua (Love China), as she had arrived on the very auspicious Double Seventh, the seventh day of the seventh month.

A colleague came down with meningitis and lay critically ill in an upstairs room, unable to be moved. On a Sunday morning, when the air alert sounded, her fellow missionaries gathered in the room with her. God's unseen shield of protection was over the little group, seemingly so powerless. A huge aerial torpedo crashed past the eaves of the house into the vegetable garden, blowing a crater thirty feet by fifteen, but harming nobody.

Even more marvellous was the discovery that a parcel containing the very first "wonder drug" had arrived at the city customs office. Refugees often carried medicines to exchange for currency. In this way Prontosil became available. The local doctor succeeded in procuring some to treat the sick woman who eventually recovered to serve the Lord for many more years.

Air alarms continued to be terrifying. Everyone had to be careful not to display anything white or to hang out white washing if they didn't want to be suspected of signalling to enemy planes. The doctor had two large white dogs that, at the sound of the alarm, would race to the roof top and begin barking. These he dyed green lest he be thought a spy!

On Amy's desk was a small printed card which simply read, "Not a single shaft can hit till the love of God sees fit." Time and again, as the bombs fell, this comforting truth brought peace of mind.

All the while, the flow of refugees fleeing westward before the Japanese advance increased. Not only did Norman and Amy have to care for extra CIM folk but many other westerners as well, including missionaries from different societies, embassy and military personnel, journalists and businessmen. All required hospitality and practical help of one kind or another.

With half the country in Japanese hands, including the CIM headquarters in Shanghai, the financial situation was chaotic and Norman's job as mission treasurer for the area became a tremendous burden. There was no banking system then. Businessmen, fearing to carry cash when they travelled to Shanghai to buy goods, would pay money locally to someone with links in the port city, and then carry letters of credit which would there be exchanged for cash. For the mission, this system worked very well under normal conditions. But the fluctuations of war could upset things and scare merchants away from trading with Shanghai.

Once when this happened, it was close to Chinese New Year when all business traditionally folded up for fifteen days. Norman was desperate for money. None of his usual contacts would do business. He himself was being presented with letters of credit from outlying stations which he was unable to honour.

He fell on his knees. "Lord, You see the situation we are in. You are our Provider. We look to You."

Just two days before Chinese New Year, a small boy presented himself at the gate. He carried the customary square of blue cloth. When the gatekeeper ushered him in, he gave Norman the card of a big businessman and delivered his message: "Your financial difficulty has come to my ears. Please accept what I have sent until times return to normal and the New Year business halt is over." The bundle contained several hundred thousands of Chinese dollars! The man was not a Christian. There was no bond, no signed agreement — just a Chinese word meaning friendship or fellowship!

So God tried and strengthened their faith. Courage, perseverance and initiative were also severely tested by the mounting problems. But God was in them all, toughening and maturing His servants through trial, preparing them for even greater responsibilities ahead. This was to be a recurring pattern throughout their lives. Repeatedly, the Lord had to use crises and emergencies to thrust them into positions of responsibility that stretched them far beyond their realized capabilities. For reluctant Norman, this also meant being pushed into situations where he had to exert a degree of leadership. All these things came unsought and indeed, unwanted. But because the word "can't" had been buried by faith, God was able to do great things through these two quite ordinary people.

To add to the strain of those Hanzhong days, Norman had his first experience of falling out of favour with mission leaders, at least at the local level. When he took over the accounts, the monthly trial balance included one item, "Error . . . $4.23," and so the books balanced! It was, admittedly, a tiny amount, but with characteristic thoroughness, Norman set about to find the cause. He and another missionary spent many hours in the dugout during air raids checking and cross-checking the accounts for months back. They finally unearthed the fact that the above small item was but the difference between a number of debits and credits amounting to considerable sums of money . . . resulting in joy for some and gloom for others!

It was a jolt to him when this exercise, instead of being appreciated by his predecessor, was taken as a personal attack, and the report that went to headquarters about him was coloured accordingly. It is possible, of course, that his own attitude may have lacked somewhat in grace and tact.

A similar, but more serious incident occurred some time later. A fellow missionary got into deep trouble and was in danger of making a mistake that would have been disastrous for himself and a national. It would also have ruined his own very effective ministry. Norman could see he was being forced into a premature decision by the unreasonable and impossible demands of the local mission leader. The poor fellow needed friendship and practical help in his dilemma, not censure. Norman gave him this and the situation was happily resolved.

Later, however, when the leader found out about it, he was furious. He severely condemned Norman and filed a black report on his attitude and conduct to headquarters, a copy of which eventually reached the Home Council in New Zealand! Fortunately for his peace of mind, Norman didn't discover this until years later. Were it not for spiritual leaders, wise in the ways of God and men, such a report would have prevented his return to China after his first furlough.

The flow of refugees brought some very special people into their lives. First came CIMer Kathleen Heath and her fellow worker, Lu Ming Ying, from Shanxi. Here was no "missionary and her Bible woman!" These two worked together in complete equality, very avant-garde for 1941. In those days, the general relationship of missionary to national was expressed by the titles given to the western missionary, whether he or she was more experienced or not. The man was *Mu Shi* (shepherd, pastor) and the lady was *Jiao Shir* (teacher). In spite of the mutual love and fellowship between westerner and national, the missionary was thus placed on a higher level.

Then along came Guo Lin Hua, another Chinese Christian worker of the new kind. Fresh, vital and totally devoted to Christ, this man was an exceptional Bible teacher with great gifts of leadership. To him all fellow workers were either "brother" or "sister," appreciated and respected for what they were, not because of any missionary status. He was somewhat suspect by the old-time church leaders who feared him, and he certainly made some of the missionaries rather uncomfortable.

Yuan Wei Yong was yet another of Christ's disciples who impressed them profoundly. This young university graduate had been disowned by her wealthy family when she gave her all to Christ and entered the Shanghai Bible Institute. She was refined and sensitive, beautiful with the fragrance of the Lord Jesus.

Through close contact, the Macs grew to love and respect these folk. They shed forever any tendency to view themselves as "senior missionaries" and, with a truer humility, placed themselves as learners at the feet of these outstanding Chinese. Norman's warm and appreciative relationship with national workers was one of the strengths of his ministry from that time on.

Inevitably, however, the strain of these years began to take its toll and both Norman and Amy were reaching the point of collapse when the Superintendent and his wife returned to relieve them. The mission leaders sent them on an extended vacation to Baoning, Sichuan, where I had been born.

They had only been there a few days when an urgent telegram arrived. Would the McIntoshes be prepared to go to the CIM hospital in Lanzhou, Gansu? Norman was needed there as business manager.

The mission had established this hospital in the Muslim northwest in memory of William Borden, a young American millionaire and graduate of Yale University, who had set out to serve among Muslims. In order to prepare himself better for this ministry by studying Arabic, Borden had stopped off at Egypt en route to China. But he had died there of a virulent disease, and his vast wealth was subsequently distributed among missions around the world. Some of it was used to build the Borden Memorial Hospital (BMH).

Tired and all as they were, Norman and Amy were thrilled with this request. Lanzhou, the strategic capital of China's great northwest, was eight hundred miles nearer to Tibet! This city, on the banks of the Yellow River, at an altitude of 5,000 feet, was at the hub of crossroads that spread out to the remotest borders of China's hinterland.

The BMH served people of many races. In fact, as the Macs were excited to learn, a whole block of buildings at the hospital was reserved specifically for receiving and treating Tibetan patients.

Norman and Amy finished their holiday and, much refreshed, returned to Hanzhong to prepare for their new assignment. With singing hearts they rejoiced that, at last, the Lord was leading them to the very threshold of the land for which they had so long felt a special concern.

CHAPTER 6

THE TONGUE-TIED PREACHER

$\mathbf{A}$ long journey overland through inland China was never easy at the best of times but, with the country at war, all normal transportation had been commandeered or was seriously disrupted. How was a family with two small children and expecting a third to get to Lanzhou?

Yet God's call had come clearly. The Macs believed that somehow He would provide a way, yet all Norman's inquiries proved fruitless. What were they to do? They packed their boxes and sat down to wait. At least they'd be ready to move as soon as anything turned up.

One Sunday afternoon, Norman went for a stroll with the local evangelist. On the edge of town they came on a crowd of people milling around someone. As they came nearer, they saw, to their surprise, that the centre of attraction was a westerner — of all people, a Royal Air Force officer. This was more than a thousand miles from the coast of China, in an area where a white face was a rarity. For a moment, the two foreigners stared at each other in amazement, the officer in his blue-grey uniform and Norman in his blue, Chinese gown.

"What on earth are you doing here?" gasped Norman. The harassed-looking officer, obviously very relieved to see him, started to explain.

It transpired that he was in charge of a convoy of RAF trucks making a goodwill mission to transport oil for the Chinese Government. This group of ground crew men had come into China after the fall of Burma, when the air crews left.

"Of course we have interpreters with us," the man went on, "but the rascals have run off on their own affairs and left me stranded. I'm trying to tell these people that all I want is to buy food and vegetables. Can you help me?"

"I'd be happy to," answered Norman, glad that he'd arrived in time to prevent the crowd molesting the man. The people were very suspicious of strangers, especially in war time.

As he helped the officer with his purchases, he learned that more than a dozen trucks were parked on the highway, out of sight of the city. There were 28 men in the convoy.

"Where are you going?" asked Norman.

"To Lanzhou" replied Commander Goddard, "wherever that might be!"

"Oh, that's interesting," said Norman quickly, "we're wanting to go there too!"

"Well, why not come along with us?" returned the officer. "We'll squeeze you in somewhere."

Early the next morning a truck picked up the family and our baggage and took us out to the waiting convoy.

For a week we lived as guests of the British Government — all expenses paid! Every night the men pitched a tent for us. Every day we joined the line-up for field rations, and enjoyed such almost-forgotten luxuries as butter and cheese. In turn Norman acted as liaison with the Chinese and was able to explain details to the soldiers that prevented them unwittingly precipitating "situations."

These lonely men, far from home, loved having two children with them. Pictures of their own families were brought out and confidences exchanged.

A sharp watch was kept for enemy attacks. Whenever planes were heard approaching, the trucks scattered rapidly and hid in shadows until it was safe to proceed again.

The convoy had intended to make three trips in all, but, as the Macs discovered later, this was the only one that took place. Norman and Amy like to tell how God wanted His servants at the BMH and so provided a Royal Air Force escort to convey them there!

On the eighth day, we arrived at the walled city of Lanzhou. Norman and Amy had read most of the available books on the northwest. Now they saw for themselves what a cosmopolitan place Lanzhou was. People of many nationalities walked its streets. From far and near came merchant traders. Great camel trains crossed the old Ghengis Khan routes and unloaded their wares on the banks of the Yellow River.

This powerful river separated the hospital from the city. As the Macs found out in due time, the usual way to commute between the two was by coracle. These were small rafts made of inflated sheepskins lashed together — very flimsy and very nerve-racking, but they did the job.

Soon it would be winter, when the great waterway would freeze several feet deep from bank to bank. Then we would walk across. About halfway was a place where we could clearly hear the roaring waters underneath. Scared, we always hurried to get past that point.

But at this season, the river was still flowing. A truck was detailed off to deliver the McIntosh family to the Borden Memorial Hospital. We drove over the large road bridge which was much further upstream.

The hospital was a sprawling affair built on rising ground from the river bank. The buildings were constructed of sun-dried mud brick and a thick mud brick wall surrounded the whole. When the truck drew closer, we noticed a single telephone wire looped over the river to the city. This kept the hospital in contact with the CIM compound which happened to be directly behind the city wall opposite.

As we drove through the main gateway of the hospital, my parents were startled to see a row of large Chinese characters which read, "Turn ye, Turn ye, why will ye die?" Who, they wondered, had chosen this singularly inappropriate inscription? It was fortunate that many of the patients who entered these portals would be illiterate!

In the business manager's house two guest rooms were reserved for western patients. It would be Amy's responsibility to care for these. Through the next year or so, she enjoyed nursing a number of interesting people, by no means all missionaries. Often non-Christian westerners came for treatment and Amy, her outside activities inevitably curtailed by small children, was grateful that God gave her a vital ministry right in the home.

A couple of months after we settled in at BMH, the first McIntosh son was born. The Chinese, by way of blessing, gave him the name of Kan-Lin, meaning "Long continued showers on the dry land." Our parents named him Alastair Morrison, after dear Bob Morrison to whom Norman owed so much.

Immediately upon arrival, Norman had set off on a tour of the compound. He was rather daunted by the size and complexity of his responsibilities. In the administration block were the operating theatre, a chapel and the Outpatient Department. There were about eighty beds in the main men's and women's wings. Also, connected to the hospital, was the leprosarium with some ninety long-term patients. A miscellany of other buildings included large kitchens, store rooms and staff housing.

As he moved about, he noted the personnel that kept this place functioning. Besides the medical staff, were all the cleaners, coolies, water-carriers, laundrymen, cooks and brick makers. These last made the fuel bricks, a mixture of coal dust and clay. *And I, Norman McIntosh,* he quaked, *am responsible for the smooth running of all this lot!*

He felt desperately inadequate. Without the experience gained as Local Secretary in South Shaanxi this bigger job as hospital accountant and administrator would have been quite beyond him. As it was, he was once more stretched beyond his known limits, and further dormant gifts and talents were developed.

This time the Lord challenged him to grow in the area of personnel management. He had no natural flair for administration and was thrown in heavy dependence upon God as he endeavoured to steer a harmonious course through staff meetings and learned to handle delicate issues in the missionary community diplomatically. Frequently there was friction among staff and Norman prayed for wisdom and patience in resolving conflicts. Most importantly, he learned something of the art of maintaining good relationships with the Chinese workers at all levels. In this he was ably assisted by the Chinese business manager.

One of his big regrets on leaving Shiquan been that he would have no more opportunity to study Chinese. Neither at Hanzhong nor at Lanzhou had he time for formal language study but, by the very nature of his job, he was forced to talk with all sorts of people and, consequently, became fluent in colloquial Chinese.

Another of his responsibilities was for hospital evangelism and this pushed him to the wall in another way.

He always had a poor opinion of himself as a preacher, and until now had avoided this responsibility whenever he could pass it on to someone else. Especially was this so when he was expected to speak in front of other missionaries who he considered were more able than he. He despaired over his inability to develop a logical sermon outline and to produce a lucid and meaningful message and he envied those who seemed to find it no difficulty. He believed himself to be a slow and unoriginal thinker.

But it was now that the Lord began to deal with him on this issue. He showed him that, to a great extent, his hesitancy was due to pride. He was more concerned to impress, attract and please others than to be God's messenger to lost and needy men. His real problem, therefore, was not a stumbling tongue but a stumbling spirit.

The time came when, in desperation, he surrendered this whole area of his life to the Lord, accepting from Him the empowering of the Holy Spirit. Then everything changed!

At last he realized in experience what he had previously acknowledged as truth, that it is God's Word alone that contains life-changing power, not the brilliance or excellence of his own material or delivery. Thankfully, this led him into a totally new experience of joy in expository preaching. He was able to minister to fellow missionaries and staff without self-consciousness and to share the gospel more freely with the men and women around him.

The response was immediate as people with hungry hearts reached out towards him. From then on there were frequent requests for him to speak at prayer meetings and other gatherings.

The spiritual gifts of preaching and leadership were bestowed on him at this time and, through the years, they have continued to develop. An original thinker he might not be but, by the Spirit's power, Norman is able to take the insights of other men, make them his own, and then preach them with such conviction and inspiration that they touch the hearts and wills of his listeners. Many times also, fresh understanding is given to him directly by the Spirit as, daily, he opens the Word in the Author's presence.

After a year or so at BMH, the Macs were granted furlough. The journey back to New Zealand involved a hazardous flight over "The Hump" (the Southern Himalayas) to Calcutta, India. Because of enemy attacks, ours was the last flight by day. Subsequent flights were taken by night. We flew in a DC-3 plane, and suffered considerably from cold and lack of oxygen in the high altitude. In the unpressurized cabin, we children sucked lollies energetically but still wailed miserably with earache.

At Calcutta we were fortunate to get a passage to Australia on a Dutch freighter, travelling in an armed convoy. There was acute danger in the Bay of Bengal where many ships had been sunk, but the freighter was spared. When we were approaching Fremantle in W. Australia, a large submarine surfaced close by causing consternation. But alarm changed to relief when it turned out to be an ally.

Some days later, as our ship neared Sydney, a radio was switched on for the first time. A band was playing "Waltzing

Matilda!" The passengers whooped with joy and all of us, adults and children, danced around wildly, relieving our feelings. Next morning a plane came out to welcome the vessel and did the victory roll round and round us. Another one safe in port!

As our freighter was piloted to her berth, it drew in behind another large merchantman, the stern of which had been blown off by enemy attack. In one cabin of the Dutch vessel, a father, mother and three little children paused before disembarking to thank God for His protection through yet another stage of their journey. So far, we had been travelling for one month.

In Sydney, Alastair had his first birthday while we awaited transport on to New Zealand. This we finally secured on a troopship in which a few jerry-built cabins housed the civilian passengers. Mother always dreaded sea voyages because she was such a poor sailor. The Tasman Sea was very rough and, to complicate matters, she was again several months pregnant. So, for most of the voyage she lay on her bunk green and ill. Consequently, Alastair was not always as closely watched as usual.

Every afternoon, cans of boiling wash water were left outside each "cabin." Alastair managed to slide across the floor unseen and pull one of these over himself. He was badly scalded. For five days, while the ship zigzagged to avoid possible submarines, he lay semi comatose. After the ship berthed, he was admitted to Wellington hospital because the burns had turned septic. But, in the goodness of God, they soon healed.

And so began our long-looked-for furlough!

To Norman and Amy's sorrow, both Dad McIntosh and Dad Lascelles had died while they were in China and would never see these grandchildren. Amy's mother, a widow once again, welcomed us eagerly.

Somehow, she managed to cram us all into her Auckland home, and a few months later, another son was received into the family. He was Gavin Heath (Chinese name, Xi-An = Joy and Peace), named for Kathleen Heath, the loved fellow worker who had shared so many weary hours with our family in the Hanchung dugout and had always been such a spiritual inspiration. Seven strenuous years in China had taken their toll in health, and Norman and Amy were emotionally exhausted. After the first excitement of welcome was over, they both became very depressed.

Amy had gone to China willing for anything. With cheerful determination she had done whatever the Lord asked her to do whether she felt she was gifted for it or not, whether she felt it was personally satisfying or not.

Many times it was not. Like other keen-minded women who give themselves to mothering small children, she was often frustrated by the lack of intellectual stimulation. For a number of years there was little time for general reading, much less serious Bible study. Language study had taken up most of her mental energy.

Now she was nervously wrung out and feeling a spiritual failure. At first, when asked to speak at meetings, she cringed because she believed she'd achieved so little that was worth sharing.

After one meeting, a well-meaning woman bustled up to her and said earnestly, "My dear, I trust you have always maintained your daily devotional times!" Tears welled into her eyes. Of course she hadn't! She needed no accuser either; she was quick enough to judge herself. With four active children under the age of five who, like their father, got up with the dawn, she had difficulty in finding any time at all to be alone. But, disheartened as she was, she realized that the Lord did not condemn. "He gently leads those that have young" (Isaiah 40:11). How lovingly He had done just that through those stressful years and surely He would restore her soul again now.

Norman also went through a dark period of doubt and discouragement. As he reviewed the years in China, he started to question the value of it all. Had *any* good been achieved?

"You're wasting your life," lied the Tempter. "How little fruit there was, in actual fact, for all that sacrifice and hardship. Stay at home now. You have surely done your bit!"

The War was still on and men Norman's age were in the armed forces fighting for their country. Influenced by this, and the knowledge that the CIM was in financial need, he decided to find a job. He couldn't bear to be a "passenger." It was, after all, his responsibility to support his own family. A job, he felt, would restore his self-respect and also relieve the mission of their keep. He started to make inquiries and received several good offers. The most attractive was to become a salesman for Tucker's Sunshine Food Products, a job with a two-storeyed house thrown in. He'd enjoy both!

Why then did he have no peace about it? Surely this was the most sensible and unselfish course to take.

One day Mr Sanders met him in a restaurant. Noticing the younger man's troubled face, he asked, "What's the matter, Norm? Can I help?" Soon Norman was pouring all his doubts and fears into the ears of this wise and understanding man.

"Norman," he said, "you have put your hand to the plough. Can you now turn back? Don't let doubt or circumstances, or even unselfishness, dictate your decisions. Have you asked the Lord's direction in this matter?"

Norman realized that he hadn't. It had just seemed to him to be the best thing to do.

Mr Sanders continued. "The Lord and the mission might be better served by your taking up a deputation ministry. Think and pray about this possibility."

Norman quailed. *I can't do all that speaking*, was his unspoken response.

"Can't?" queried the Master. "Haven't I anointed your tongue?"

As Norman and Amy prayed about it, God confirmed this to be His will, and peace of heart was restored. At home or abroad, they were in the Lord's service still. In consultation with the mission, it was decided that Norman should go on full-scale deputation, concentrating mainly on the far south of

New Zealand.

So, at the end of 1944, our family of six squeezed into a newly-acquired Austin-7, nicknamed for its size, "Zaccheus," and set off on the a thousand-mile drive to Dunedin in the South Island. Here, for three months, we were the guests of a Christian businessman, Mr Adam Paterson, and enjoyed the luxury of his beautiful big home. Here too, I started school and Dad started deputation.

Then we were loaned a home by the McSkimming family in the little village of Benhar, three miles out of Balclutha. In the main, Mother stayed put with us children while Dad, on the go all the time, ranged far and wide throughout Otago, Southland and Fiordland, making the needs of God's work in China widely known. For long stretches of time, Amy was a solo parent. When fatigue and self-pity threatened to dampen her spirit, she reminded herself that "can't" was dead and mustn't be resurrected now. She clung to the Lord and found that when she couldn't, He could.

In deputation of this sort, Norman was, in a sense, his own master and could work as much or as little as he pleased. He recognized the danger in this. *If I were in a secular job*, he cautioned himself, *I'd be required to work full-time and hard. Can I offer my divine Master anything less?* Conscientiously therefore, he filled his days and evenings with visiting and meetings and worked very hard.

The sheer repetitiveness of deputation work, though, threatened to make his ministry dry and mechanical. He soon realized that to maintain vitality, he needed to safeguard his devotional life. Sleeping in different homes all the time made this more difficult. But, before he retired each evening, he ensured that he knew where the hostess kept teapot and matches.

Before dawn, he'd be prowling around the kitchen, lighting up the stove and brewing a cup of tea. Most hostesses were delighted to enter a warm kitchen when, later, they came to prepare breakfast.

Norman made himself one of the family wherever he

stayed. He filled coal buckets, split kindling, washed dishes or anything else he saw needed doing. He refused to be waited on and made a special point of getting alongside every member of the family, including the children. Consequently, he was a popular guest.

It didn't take him long to discover that everywhere he went there was deep spiritual hunger. Even here in New Zealand he was still to be God's messenger pointing men and women to Jesus Christ. Often this was done on an individual basis as he talked with folk in their homes.

In his meetings he made sure there was always a personal spiritual challenge. The Holy Spirit led him, largely through trial and error, to develop a very effective pattern of deputation.

Little one or two-teacher schools were common throughout the countryside in those days. Norman would go first to the local school and offer to give a social studies talk on China. This offer was usually snapped up, but with the proviso, "No religion, mind!" He gave his word and faithfully kept it. But, would the teacher allow him to tell about the place and time of his lantern lecture that night in the township? Why, certainly!

So, night after night saw crowded halls, full of enthusiastic children *and* their parents. There they heard that "God so loved the world that He gave His only Son . . ." and saw pictures of people in other lands who had found life in Christ.

On one such school visit, Norman met a headmaster who was decidedly cold to his friendly approach.

"All right," the man agreed reluctantly, "you can have just ten minutes!" But at the end of that time, during which the whole school had listened spellbound, the headmaster signalled for Norman to continue. The children were enthralled as Norman went on and on.

When it came to morning break, the headmaster invited him to come across to the schoolhouse for a cup of tea. There he met the teacher's wife and the three of them had a friendly chat.

As he was about to leave, Norman asked the couple if they would like to have a short prayer together. They agreed. No sooner had he opened his mouth to pray, than the wife broke down and wept. Then the husband did the same and, that morning, two backsliders returned to the Lord. From that day on they became wholehearted supporters of the Lord's missionary endeavour. Years later, they farewelled their own two daughters off to Africa as missionaries.

Sometimes though, Norman would find meetings a real struggle. One such was when he spoke at the Otago University Evangelical Union. Addressing university students always made him nervous anyway, but this meeting was a disaster. While he was speaking, several fellows barged in to drag out the piano. Students passed in a constant stream through one corner of the room and a band was practising overhead. Norman went back to the home where he was staying almost crying with discouragement. He felt he was a complete failure and should never speak again!

However, he had to speak again. The next Sunday found him preaching in a Dunedin church. After the service a young man approached him.

"I'm not a member of this church," he said. "I heard you speak at the Evangelical Union on Thursday and inquired where you'd be preaching today. I have to talk to you."

This young medical student had been deeply moved by what he had heard. As Norman talked with him further, he surrendered his life to Christ, offering himself unconditionally for missionary service if God so willed.

On this first furlough, Norman sold large quantities of mission literature and took in over a thousand subscriptions for *China's Millions*, the monthly CIM periodical. Through his ministry, he saw many men, women and children come to the Saviour and his heart rejoiced. Widespread interest in China and the CIM was generated and hundreds of formerly unconcerned people pledged their prayers.

This increased support was going to be essential as, after the War, CIM missionaries returned for what was to be their last and most difficult term of service in the land of China.

Norman travelled thousands of miles in the little Austin-7, but fuel was strictly rationed. "Zaccheus" carried an empty jeep can, dubbed by Norman "The Widow's Cruse." Through the generosity of farmers who donated petrol from their own precious quotas, the Lord kept His servant on the road.

Great joy came to the whole family with the birth of the fifth child, Iona Paterson (Chinese name, Ai-lien = Love-link). She was named for the Paterson family to whom we all owed so much love and kindness. The new baby was soon nicknamed "Twinkle" because of her dancing eyes and active hands and feet.

With the end of the War, the McIntoshes started praying that the way would quickly open for them to return to China. After some months, word came that a few men missionaries were being called back to the field for urgent ministry. Then came the summons for everybody to prepare to return.

There was so much to get ready. Amy, knee deep in toddlers and diapers, felt overwhelmed. Most of the children's clothes would have to be made. We two older girls would be going to Chefoo boarding school. Extensive outfits had to be put together for us and name tags sewn on everything.

"Father," Amy cried desperately, "I need help!"

There was a knock at the door. The post girl handed in a parcel. In it was some children's clothing. Unknown friends in the far north, hearing that the Macs were returning to China, had sent two pairs of little boys' trousers — blue to match their eyes, and a perfect fit for Alastair and Gavin. How Amy thanked the Lord for that gift!

But that wasn't all. The same day, in the afternoon, a parcel was delivered from the far south. In it were two shirts for the boys — beautifully sewn, a perfect fit, and exactly the same colour as the trousers received earlier in the day!

"Well," gasped Amy with amazement, "if God can plan a suit for each of the boys, supplied by people unknown to each other and hundreds of miles apart, who am I to worry?" She sang around the house that day and somehow, after that, preparations went more smoothly.

When Averil and I later arrived at school and our things were unpacked, one of the staff members exclaimed, "What beautiful outfits. These are the sort of people who ought to have large families!" Forty years later, I still have in my possession a towel (once plain white) which Mother sent with me to Chefoo. Besides a neatly sewn name tag is the embroidered number "14" in blue (the girls' colour; the boys had red numbers), so that the laundry workers, unable to read English, would be able to sort the washing. On the border of the towel is a daintily embroidered clump of forget-me-nots!

Norman was wanted back at the Borden Memorial Hospital as business manager. It was early 1947 and the day of departure had been set. We had been three years in the homeland. As Norman and Amy prepared to return to northwest China, a long-buried question resurfaced in their minds. *Will God at this time open the way for us to go into Tibet?*

CHAPTER 7

VISION BECOMES REALITY

As the Macs waited in the queue to go up the ship's gangway at Auckland, a man in front of Norman opened the daily newspaper. Large headlines screamed, "PLANE CRASH IN CHINA! THREE CIM MISSIONARIES KILLED!" Cold fear clutched at their hearts.

"We're fools to be going back to China!" they thought in sudden panic. "What are we thinking of to be taking five little children into a country still in the chaos of war?"

But the Voice of encouragement spoke quietly in their souls, "Peace, be still." The swelling waves of anxiety subsided and their spirits calmed. They were in the Master's will and He could be trusted.

At Sydney, they changed ships. The old New Zealand inter-island ferry, the *S.S. Maori*, had been sold to an eastern shipping company and was renamed the *S.S. Hwalien*. The Macs, with others returning to China, had expected to leave on her right away, but found on arrival that she was not ready to sail.

"She will be ready in a few days," they were assured. But days lengthened into weeks and weeks into two interminable months before they were finally called up. Expecting each day to be the last, they had remained cooped up in impossibly crowded lodgings. As the group included many young children, nerves had worn thin by the time they set sail.

Nearly thirty CIMers were among the passengers that embarked on what should have been a carefree, restful journey. It turned out to be the very opposite. The reason soon became obvious. The captain, who had been commissioned to deliver the ship to the East, naturally considered that he was in charge. But the new owners had placed on board their representative who also held a captain's ticket. He felt that he was in charge. This clash of leadership meant that the crew didn't know from whom they were taking orders, and the result was an unhappy ship. The crew was mutinous and the passengers in a constant state of anxiety.

They limped into port after port and there was an air of uncertainty at every place. It was an incredible situation. That the ship finally arrived at its destination without a major blow-up was probably due to the prayers of the Lord's people on board.

For missionaries who would be living and working in teams, it was a vivid object lesson. Coincidentally, at their next workers' conference in Lanzhou, Mr J O Sanders (then the CIM Director for Australia), spoke on the vital need for a team of God's servants to work together in love and harmony if God is to be glorified.

"What would I do on this hospital compound if I were the devil?" he asked. "I would work overtime at sowing discord among the brethren."

Thirty years later, when Averil was a missionary in Thailand, Rev. John Stott was the guest speaker at their field conference. He addressed the same theme. "Today," he began, "I want to speak to you about your greatest problem — your fellow missionary!"

The *S.S. Hwalien* crawled into Shanghai on 8 May 1947, eleven years after Norman and Amy had first landed there. It was exciting to unpack boxes of personal belongings that had been stored in a neutral warehouse throughout the war years. Nostalgically, Amy unearthed her unused wedding gown. Norman was delighted to get his hands on his carpentry kit once more.

The CIM headquarters was bulging at the seams as workers poured back into China. To add to the congestion, the Chefoo School was also temporarily housed there while more suitable premises were being sought. Averil and I, now aged six and eight, were to be left there when the rest of the family went on inland.

Ever since the birth of their children, the thought of parting from them had hung over Norman and Amy like a dark shadow. Again and again, personal battles had to be fought over the matter. The flesh wept, "I can't!" but the spirit took hold of God by faith and tremblingly affirmed, "Your will be done, in this as in everything else." It was the hardest sacrifice of their missionary career to surrender their precious children into the hands of others and to go so far away from them. To exercise faith for themselves was one thing, to exercise it for their children was quite another.

All too soon the long-dreaded moment arrived.

Typically, Amy kept everyone cheerful and occupied until final goodbyes were said. She knew we girls would quickly settle down once she and Dad were out of the way, and could see no value in allowing us all to wallow in emotion until we worked ourselves into a frenzy.

But, as the plane left the tarmac and started on the nine hours' flight inland, her pent-up feelings burst through all restraint and she wept for her little ones. The Word that came over and over to comfort her heart was, "*He* is worthy for whom you should do this."

Norman also suffered acutely at these partings. Years later, when we children were older and had to be left in New Zealand for high school, the anticipated time of separation was three years! After saying "Goodbye" to us, he fled to the home of a good friend. Subsequently, a daughter of that home commented, "I never saw a man cry like that before. He came in and said, 'We've left the children!' then broke down and sobbed and sobbed!"

Back at Lanzhou, Amy had to force herself to make any kind of a home. Without the girls there was no interest and she went around listlessly for weeks feeling as though something had died within her. One morning, as she was taking devotions for some leprosy patients in their chapel, she looked out of the window and noticed the three new graves of westerners who had died while they'd been away on furlough. One was the grave of a baby. Under the name was inscribed a single word — *Safe*.

"Safe!" The word echoed in Amy's heart. "Your girls are safe too, whatever happens, perfectly safe in My keeping." Her drooping spirits started to revive.

Norman plunged back into his work at the hospital. He soon found his days so crowded that he was scarcely able to spend any time at home. To speed up bookkeeping, he mastered the intricacies of the abacus, and thereafter did all the hospital accounts with the aid of this ancient calculator.

As in Hanzhong, the effects of war and civil unrest added immeasurable strain to Norman's regular responsibilities. The Communists were pressing their advantage throughout the war-torn country and were daily gaining ground with the common people. Renewed anti-foreign feeling was abroad and much fear and uncertainty prevailed at every level of society. At BMH there was unexpected trouble with servants and staff.

One day, a youth was brought into the hospital seriously ill. As was so often the case, he had been unsuccessfully treated by unqualified local doctors first. Then, when he was clearly dying, he was brought to the western hospital. While realizing it was probably too late, the doctor still operated in a last-ditch effort to save his life, but the lad died. The troublemakers infiltrating society at that time used this opportunity to stir up feeling against the Christian hospital. They accused the doctor of murder!

What was to be done? The missionaries prayed for guidance. Obviously the body must be inspected by an authority from the Chinese Medical Association to prove there had been no malpractice. Until such a person could be found, however, they would have to prevent the body leaving the hospital. All too well they knew there would be attempts by evil men to steal it away and mutilate it as "evidence" against the foreign doctor.

The corpse was locked in the mortuary, and then guarded around the clock by the foreigners. The Chinese staff couldn't be asked to take part in this as bribery or coercion might well have proved too much for them. It was midwinter, so the body was, fortunately, frozen. But very nearly frozen too were the poor men who had to stand watch over it day and night for many weeks.

As business manager, much of the burden of all this fell on Norman. He was under constant pressure from relatives and local officials to release the body. One day, he was literally "back to the wall," facing a hundred or so angry men who came thirsting for blood. Somehow he was able to fend them off, but after they left, he found himself trembling violently. How much longer could they all stand this strain?

Finally, in answer to prayer, they were able to hand the body over to responsible authorities. Still the tension wasn't over. The case dragged on and on. But eventually the doctor was exonerated. The missionary community breathed a sigh of relief and thanksgiving to the Lord for His protection through what could have become a very ugly situation.

This incident was no chance case, however, but a straw in the wind of change that would in the next two or three years reach gale force throughout the land. It was the grim harbinger of things to come.

Once again the financial situation became chaotic and inflation soared. There were acute shortages of flour and wheat (the staple food of north China). Norman was sometimes driven to the point of desperation as he sought to keep everyone in the hospital fed and to meet the monthly wage bill.

"At times, I ask myself why I had to return to this type of work," he wrote to Mother Lascelles, "for the strain of it all, plus the food shortages and financial stringency, is just getting me down. I am afraid I have not yet learned to rest in Him completely."

But he did trust the Lord. He had to! And time and again

he was awed at the unexpected way the Divine Provider supplied their recurring needs.

Because of runaway inflation, the staff would no longer accept their wages in paper money alone. Norman had to pay them a certain measure of flour also. He bought wheat and ground it. But there came a day when there was no wheat to be had. The military had commandeered all local supplies. Norman called the whole community to prayer.

The next morning, a huge lorry pulled into the compound loaded with wheat! A missionary in a town north of Lanzhou had happened on a large store. Knowing of their perennial need for grain, he had, on his own initiative, purchased a truckload and sent it down unannounced.

Then there were endless problems in obtaining medical supplies. When they visited Shanghai later that year, Norman and Dr Clarke set out on a urgent search for drugs and medical equipment. "Lord, please help us to find the things we need so critically," was their prayer.

An encounter with an official of the American Red Cross resulted in the unbelievable donation of an X-ray unit, a large shipment of excess army medical units, plus drugs and other equipment. It was a miracle of supply! Nor did the Lord stop there. The Red Cross shipped the whole consignment right across China to Lanzhou, by air!

That year Norman had a close brush with death. The far northwest was generally very dry. But one evening there was a sudden, terrific thunderstorm with torrential rain that caused a lot of damage to mud walls and roofs. As soon as the downpour started, Norman, clad in oilskin and gumboots, went on a tour of inspection around the hospital. Others of the staff also turned out with spades, shovels and sticks in an endeavour to control the water which was fast gouging holes and trenches through the fine loess soil.

Norman was inspecting a section of the rear outer wall, which stood about twenty feet high, when he noticed a slight movement. Instinctively he stepped back a pace or two. Simultaneously the wall collapsed and tons of earth and rock crashed down where he had been standing and right up to his feet. He was completely hidden in the cloud of dust. One of the doctors who saw it, was sure that he had been buried underneath. When he knew that Norman had escaped, he hurried down to the house to tell Amy about what he described as no less than a miraculous deliverance.

The Lord had plans to move Norman and Amy deeper into Satan's stronghold. Could this have been a devilish attack on his life? Norman was quite shaken. One second later, and he'd have been killed. Surely God had saved his life that night. Was it a coincidence that in Auckland at that very hour, a CIM prayer group was interceding for them?

Ever since their return to China, the personal burden Norman and Amy had long felt for the Tibetan people had sharpened into an urgent and incessant call. God was stirring in their hearts and they longed to be released from the hospital for a full-time ministry to these very needy and neglected people.

While many Tibetans successfully found their way to the BMH for treatment, and there were a number of long-term Tibetan patients in the leprosarium, these had usually travelled long distances to get there and generally arrived in the most pitiable condition. The harshness of the land and the hazards they faced en route were enormous. When they were sighted, other people were likely to set their dogs on them or stone them. Once, the governor of Qinghai rounded up all the lepers he could find and had them shot.

The Tibetans as a people were riddled with disease and it was obvious that a medical work more readily available to them, right up in their own territory, would be a tremendous boon. It would also provide an effective opening for the gospel. The CIM had attempted Tibetan work before, but this witness through the years had been costly. Nine graves of missionaries and nineteen graves of missionary children in Qinghai told their own story. For various reasons, it had been impossible to keep any station manned for long at a time.

But now the CIM planned to renew the thrust into Tibet.

Norman and Amy strongly desired to be part of it. So they wrote to their prayer partners, "The CIM is planning to open a border hospital in the Tibetan foothills. Pray that if the Lord wants us to go forward there, His will shall be made very clear."

Sometime later, the glad word went out, "The Directors seem satisfied that the Lord has called us to Tibetan work, and we will probably proceed there — but nothing definite yet."

It was at this point that Norman was invited down to Shanghai to meet the band of rich and influential Chinese Christian businessmen who had formed themselves into what became known as the Holy Light Fellowship. Their object was to evangelize China's minority and frontier peoples, with a special emphasis on Tibet. They were keen to cooperate with the CIM, so Dr and Mrs Rupert Clarke and the McIntoshes were seconded to the Fellowship to open medical clinics in Tibetan territory. This border land, although largely inhabited by Tibetans, was regarded by China as part of its dominion. So the decision was made and, with joy in their hearts, Norman and Amy started to prepare themselves for this long-awaited service.

Actually, some time before this, Amy had, by faith, begun learning Tibetan. Although there were three children to care for and she was constantly called upon to give hospitality, she set about the task of studying this new language with characteristic determination. For oral practice, she talked with a Tibetan patient in the leprosarium, and was delighted when other Tibetans understood her simple questions. She studied hard, but was handicapped by the dearth of available aids. Whenever a Tibetan-speaking missionary happened to pass through Lanzhou (a rare occurrence), she took the opportunity to learn from him, even if, as in one case, what she learned came over with a strong Swedish accent! On the whole, however, she made encouraging progress.

But Norman was frustrated. Try as he would he could

find no time at all for language study. The demands of the hospital continued to swallow up all his energies. However, God was equipping His servant in other ways for the ministry ahead.

Dr Keith Cameron, a sensitive, clever, courageous but lonely man, became his friend and opened new vistas to him. One was photography. He enthused Norman and together they spent their spare moments in a hastily-constructed darkroom, developing film and printing pictures. He also knew how to develop colour film and passed on his knowledge to his disciple. This accomplishment was to be a great asset to the work in the months ahead, but for the present it provided a small relaxation from the days of strain. Norman's latent artistic ability found a satisfying outlet in this new hobby. With his natural eye for good composition, he began to produce some beautiful pictures.

Another vista that opened to him at this time was practical medicine. Seeing Norman's interest and aptitude in medical things, Keith and some of the other doctors taught him many first-aid methods for relieving suffering. He learned a good deal from watching them operate, and they allowed him to practise some of the simpler procedures under their supervision. Among other things, he learned to give injections, even intravenously, sew up wounds, aspirate hydatid cysts, pull teeth and operate on eyelids to correct damage done through ingrowing eyelashes. He became amazingly adept.

It was this medical skill that was to open for him the gateway into the vast nomadic grasslands of Tibet. God, who delights to give His children the desires of their hearts, had rekindled Norman's boyhood longing to become a doctor and intended to use this very thing to swing wide the rusty hinges of Tibet!

Well aware of the nature of the spiritual conflicts that lay ahead and of the possible shortness of time available to them, Amy prepared for the new venture by writing many articles for western magazines. She called the attention of the church to the Tibetan people and their plight and challenged Christians everywhere to pray. In those days, people were avid for news of this almost unknown land. Amy's articles, illustrated with Norman's photographs, were printed and reprinted by Christian periodicals in Britain, North America and Australasia. It was a day of opportunity.

But the Tibetan advance was bitterly attacked. Baby Twinkle fell ill. She went downhill rapidly, lost a lot of weight, and everything she swallowed went straight through undigested. Uncertain of the exact cause of the illness, the doctors put her on a fat-free diet and hoped for the best. But, for a long time, she hovered between life and death and showed no sign of improvement. Norman and Amy watched the little one anxiously and held desperately to the Lord. "This work has cost the lives of many missionary children, Lord. Why should ours be spared when others are not? Yet we look to You to heal our baby." Eventually, the corner was turned and the child gradually regained strength.

While the following incident contributed nothing to Twinkle's recovery, it did a great deal for the faith of the older children. They overheard a doctor say, "If only we could get bananas, she could eat those." So the youngsters prayed for bananas, a fruit unknown in Lanzhou.

In Shanghai, two thousand miles away, a certain director was preparing to visit the missionaries of the northwest. On his way to the airfield, he saw some bananas and thought, *I'll take them some bananas. They'll like those!* When he arrived at the BMH complete with bananas, the young Macs were thrilled, and never doubted that God had answered their prayer.

After the long strain of Twinkle's illness, the Lord gave His weary servants an unexpected joy. Because the Chefoo school had to be moved from Shanghai to its new location in Guling (a hill resort in Jiangsu Province), the Christmas vacation was to be longer than usual.

If the parents wished, their children could be sent home!

The Macs decided it was right to have the girls home, and they asked the Lord to provide the rather heavy travel expenses and suitable escorts for the journey. This He lovingly did, through some special gifts from the homeland, and the whole family was reunited for a most joyous Christmas.

It was a bitterly cold winter and the Yellow River was frozen many feet deep right across. One night, an airline pilot dropped in for a cup of tea and told them that the Gobi Desert was under snow. Ice rather than snow was more the norm around dry Lanzhou, but we children had a marvellous time with the sled Dad had made for us in his few free moments.

But all too soon the time came for our return to Chefoo. How I dreaded the thought of leaving again. I wrote to Nana, "Here is a text. I am with you all-ways . . . the school is going to Guling. We were very kroudid at Shanghai. The children that are up there say it is a lovly plase to have a school." I hoped it was, but nowhere, in my opinion, could be as nice as home.

When the day of departure finally arrived, Dad was away. He had taken the visiting Director from North America and the Superintendent on a long trip into the far northwest. It fell to Mother to see us to the airfield. She took five-year-old Alastair with her for moral support.

After the plane had left, Amy and her small escort rattled back into Lanchow in a horse-drawn cart, the usual form of public transport. Suddenly, Alastair demanded, "Sing that song to me, Mum, 'I've got joy, joy, joy, joy, down in my heart!'" Let it be recorded that she tried!

When Norman returned, the family got packed up ready to leave. The new clinic was to be established at Hualong in Qinghai Province. *At last*, they thought joyfully, *we are actually on our way to Tibet!* So it was a shock when the news came at the last moment, that the couple who were scheduled to replace them at BMH would not be returning for another year!

But God's time had come and nothing was allowed to stand in His way. This and other obstacles were overcome. Spring was well advanced and the loess countryside again mantled in beautiful green when they set out at last for the Tibetan foothills.

CHAPTER 8

ON THE ROOF OF THE WORLD

Tibet, high up on the roof of the world, was as proud and remote as an eagle on the crag. For centuries the land remained impregnable in its isolation, the combination of inhospitable terrain, bitter climate and fierce people successfully repelling all invaders. But soon, this would be changed for ever. The Chinese Red Army was to march relentlessly into the land, even to the sacred stronghold of Lhasa itself, decimating the population in the process.

As has so often happened in the past, God "shaves with a razor that is hired" (Isaiah 7:20). Atheistic Communism was to be the tool in His hand to break open this fortress whose inhabitants lived in deep spiritual darkness, enslaved body and soul by demons. Proud they might be, but they were morally degraded and physically diseased.

Before the cataclysm, however, the good news of God's salvation was to be spread far and wide among these people. But in May 1948, when Norman and Amy arrived at Hualong on the Tibetan border, there was no known Tibetan believer in any direction.

The plan was for the Macs to go as an advance guard to Hualong to get the place operational. Then the medical team would follow and open the clinic. The team would include Ruth Duncan, a nurse from Texas, and two Chinese graduate nurses from the CIM's hospital at Kaifeng in Henan. Doctors would be supplied from the BMH, one at a time on a rotational basis.

The trip from Lanzhou to Hualong took twelve hours and involved a steady climb, as the new station was situated at 10,000 feet above sea level. The air up there was so rare that the newcomers found their hearts pounding with the slightest physical exertion. They had to learn to do things more slowly.

The compound was a typical walled-in square of single-storey, flat-roofed rooms opening into a large central courtyard. This was divided across the middle by another narrow building. The back section would be kept private for the team and the front for the clinic and the use of patients. The place had been lying empty for many a long day and everything was filthy dirty and in crumbling disrepair.

"We've got a job to do here," said Norman cheerfully, stamping in and raising a cloud of dust. For days he was kept very busy with workmen doing repairs and making alterations. They plastered fresh mud on the walls and roofs outside, and whitewashed all the rooms inside. Fresh paper had to be pasted over the windows as glass panes were almost unknown in the northwest. The children loved all this activity with Dad and Mum, and playing with mud suited them fine too!

The Macs had been unable to bring any baggage with them on the jeep, so had to purchase a few rough bowls on the street to tide them over until their belongings arrived by cart ten days later. The ancient stove filled the house with smoke whenever it was lit, but Amy refused to be discouraged and worked hard to get the place pleasant and homelike.

As soon as everything was ready, they sent a message down to Lanzhou, "All clear, we're ready for action!" But week followed week and there was no sign of the team.

At Lanzhou the medics were held up by a tangle of red tape. The Superintendent and his wife decided to take Ruth, a new missionary, on ahead to get orientated. Two attempts to get to Hualong were aborted, however, as each time the jeep broke down and they had to return to the hospital.

The devil didn't want this clinic opened! Tibetan work had always been difficult and the enemy of the Light had so far been successful in obliterating the effects of the gospel. But Jesus said, "I will build my church, and the gates of hell shall not prevail against it!" (Matthew 16:18) Norman and Amy clung on to this promise and waited.

In the meantime, they became acquainted with the handful of Chinese Christian believers in the area. With the aid of Amy's new acquisition, a piano accordion, she and Norman would gather scores of children for a sing-song and a message in Chinese. Their parents, happy for a diversion, would also stand around and listen, though many people in this area were fanatical Muslims and very anti-Christian.

Two Tibetan lamas (priests) came to look around. One of them had been in BMH for surgery so felt he was an old acquaintance. Amy was most encouraged (to the point of being childishly happy!) to be able to talk with these men in their own language.

At last Norman could get down to serious language study. At this point, he, who had initially found Chinese so hard to learn, made a wonderful discovery. He was able to grasp Tibetan much more easily and soon found his fluency in the new language outstripping his ability in the old. Tibetan is a difficult language, but God who knew how short was to be the day of opportunity, gave His servant speedy mastery.

Finally, six weeks later, all the medics arrived at once, before their telegram! Dr Rupert Clarke and Ruth opened the clinic immediately and, in the first week, treated upwards of four hundred patients. By September, well over two thousand had received treatment.

The majority of patients had VD in one form or another, especially the Tibetans and Muslims. Promiscuity was the accepted way of life amongst priests and people, which accounted for the high incidence of syphilis and gonorrhoea and the very low birth rate. The Holy Light clinic was a single beacon in a vast darkness. As it became known, sick people travelled enormous distances to receive help. Some rode animals, but most came many days by foot, suffering a great deal en route. One man staggered in carrying his wife on his back and both were near collapse on arrival.

While the patients waited to see the doctor or were undergoing treatment, they lived on the compound. There were no beds. Conditions were rough and ready and patients did their own cooking over little clay braziers fuelled with dried animal dung, but at least they had a roof over their heads. Norman and Amy moved among them telling of the love of Jesus in Chinese or Tibetan.

As time went on, the flow of Tibetans to the clinic increased and many hundreds received treatment and were introduced to Jesus Christ. Not infrequently, lamas would come down from far distant monasteries seeking medical help. They returned carrying the gospel story with them into the heartlands of Tibet. None believed at that time, but the good seed was widely scattered, and the call went out to prayer partners to lay hold by faith that it would germinate in the hearts of the people and result in a great harvest.

But, busy and all as the workers were, they knew that they could not depend on the prayers of supporters alone to achieve results. Regular prayer times were augmented by days of prayer and fasting when together the team members would meet in the Lord's presence. They sought His guidance for every aspect of the work and received fresh empowering for their ministry. If a living church was ever to grow in such an arid place, it would be through prayer. As they interceded for a people who named the names of gods and demons by the score, they chose as their theme song, "Jesus, the Name high over all!" Their special emphasis was, "His only righteousness I show, His saving grace proclaim; 'Tis all my business here below to cry, 'Behold, the Lamb!'"

The Tibetans were very religious. They often asked the missionaries for a picture of Jesus, so that it could be put up with all the other images and "worshipped when we worship our gods." The truth that God is the Almighty One, and that He alone may be worshipped, was hard for them to take. In fact, this was the primary obstacle to their receiving the gospel. The Tibetan name the Christians used for God, literally translated, meant "God-than-that-there-is-no-higher."

Little by little, there were visible spiritual results from the Hualong outreach. Amy prayed with a weeping woman of 35, the daughter of one of the few Chinese Christians in the town. Later, the mother came and told Amy that, during the prayer, her daughter had believed in Jesus with her "whole heart" and was truly a changed person.

Soon a women's meeting was commenced with ten present, all Chinese. The first person to be baptized was a woman. The service was held down at the mill stream, and the tiny congregation sat on the grassy bank singing hymns of praise to the Saviour while the townspeople watched.

One by one, people were added to the church, but not from among the Tibetans or Muslims. These folk were held fast in the devil's grip and his opposition to the messengers of the Light was relentless. A Muslim woman, who had been receiving long-term medical care at the clinic, was suddenly divorced by her husband. A young Tibetan priest who professed to believe, unaccountably disappeared. This was disheartening but not unexpected. Norman and Amy had shuddered when they read how a Tibetan believer in another place had been sewn into a wet yak skin, then put out into the scorching sun to be slowly crushed and suffocated as the skin shrunk. Any Tibetans who became Christians did so at the risk of their lives.

With the probability of such persecution, it was an awesome responsibility to point these people to Christ. Norman and Amy had to keep their sights set on eternal perspectives and remind themselves constantly that without Christ the Tibetans had no hope of life at all.

The team was happy and harmonious. The devil was unable to destroy the ministry through sowing discord. But he dealt a body blow to the work when a Christian male nurse, who also spoke Tibetan, gave in to temptation and fell morally. Not only was the Christian witness damaged, but his necessary departure put a tremendous strain on their meagre

Tibetan-speaking staff. Sadly, the others saw the unrepentant man go off, and prayed that some day he would return to the Lord and to useful service once more.

Without a vehicle, the Hualong team was very isolated. When the first change of doctors occurred, Rupert set out early for Lanzhou on a bicycle! But the rain came on and he returned at supper time tired out and caked with sticky red mud, having covered a distance of only eight miles. He left again the following morning by mule to try a different route.

So there was great excitement when news came that the Holy Light Fellowship had purchased a jeep for the Hualong work and was going to fly it to Lanzhou. There was a long wait before the vehicle actually materialized, but the anticipation of its arrival helped the team endure jolting journeys and saddle sores more cheerfully.

Whenever they could be freed from the clinic, Norman and Amy took the opportunity to visit Tibetans in the district. These were mostly sedentary Tibetans who lived in separate settlements outside the town. At this stage the only nomadic Tibetans they had much to do with were those who came as patients to the clinic.

As the Mac's language teacher was a lama, this also put them into contact with several nearby lamaseries. They started to receive invitations to visit.

There were some sixty lamaseries in the Hualong — Gui-de area. These had a stranglehold on the populace because one son from every family was required to become an acolyte. Each group of lamaseries was presided over by a Living Buddha who was believed to be a reincarnation of the spirit of Buddha. When one died, an infant was sought who had been born at the exact hour of his death, a search that could take many months. It was believed that this child would be the reincarnation of the dead Buddha. The genuineness of his reincarnation would then be tested in various ways. For instance, a collection of objects, including some of the dead Buddha's belongings, would be displayed before him. If the child should reach for one that had belonged to the deceased man, it was taken as clear indication that he was the new Living Buddha. The lamas all worshipped the Living Buddha — their Rimpoche, Precious One. He received the homage that belongs to God alone.

On their first visit to a lamasery, Norman and Amy, with their teacher, arrived in time for dinner. There, seated on two beautiful carpets, they were served a meal of boiled rice, flour and raisins swimming in butter. This they ought to have washed down with scalding tea, but since about two ounces of butter floated on the top of each bowl, the visitors found it practically impossible to swallow. Later, they were to develop considerable agility in blowing the butter away and gulping a quick mouthful of tea before it floated back again!

Not only was butter a staple in the diet, but it had many other uses. In that frigid climate where people rarely washed, butter was a skin oil. Babies were carried, stark naked, in the bosom of their mothers' sheepskin gowns. Only their heads protruded, and these were kept well buttered as protection from the cold. Consequently they were caked black with dirt. The odour of rancid butter and unwashed bodies could be quite overpowering.

In the lamasery were crowds of red-robed priests and many little boy acolytes. Amy sat beside one who was only five years old! It was appalling to see these small priests-of-the-future learning all the ways of the devil from older men who were steeped in evil. Homosexuality was commonplace. Gambling and other vices were rife and the worship of spirits resulted in the horror and ugliness of demon possession. Sick at heart, Amy thought, *These children should be with their mothers, happily playing in the sunshine.*

After dinner, the visitors were ushered into the presence of the Living Buddha. He was only eighteen years old, and ruled over 28 lamaseries. Norman took many photographs of him arrayed in all his magnificent red robes. Although the Macs tried to put him at his ease, the poor young man was perspiring with nervousness, never having seen westerners before. Norman mended a clock that had stopped and presented him with an assortment of gifts, including a copy of Matthew's Gospel and a picture- story of the Good Samaritan.

The Tibetan religion is a complicated hotchpotch of animism and Buddhism. Fertility rites were important. The worship of spirits and practice of witchcraft was all-pervasive.

A sorcerer came to the kitchen door one day to ask for some hot water. As he held out his bowl to be filled, Amy was startled to see it was the top of a human skull. On inquiry, she learned that this, and the human thigh bone which dangled from the sash at his waist, were part of a sorcerer's paraphernalia. An unpleasant question nagged at her mind, *Where do they get such bones?*

It was a while before she found out. Because of the intense cold, the ground froze deep and no graves could be dug for months of the year. Disposal of a corpse was simple. It was taken to a high vantage point and dismembered. Then the priest would blow on his long, resonant horn and, apparently out of a clear blue sky, would come birds of prey. These would pick the bones clean, and so the needs of sorcerers were easily met!

Another time, an unusual Tibetan stayed at the clinic. He seemed to be part Living Buddha and part magician. His rosary was made from 108 pieces of human skull, each piece, it was claimed, having been cut from a different head. The doctor examined the bones and confirmed that they were certainly human cranium. Apparently, the beads had been big when new, but had been worn down with much praying and were by then quite small.

When the time arrived for the celebration of the Devil Dance of all Tibet, the Macs were invited to another monastery to see it. This has been widely written about, but those who report such "fantastic" things usually have no idea of the sorrow that fills the hearts of Christ's ambassadors when they witness them. The Devil Dance was noisy and colourful, exciting and even fierce in parts, but to Norman and Amy it was tragic because of the hopeless darkness it represented. Various explanations have been given of it but it has always remained something of a mystery to foreigners.

The crushing sense of evil was suffocating as time and again on these visits, the Macs saw chanting halls filled with old men and little boys worshipping a false god hour after hour. They'd come back to the clinic feeling oppressed and overwhelmed by it all. How could the Light ever penetrate such thick darkness?

Deeply burdened, Amy felt compelled to write a true-to-life story to explain the situation to western readers. *The Man in the Sheepskin* was penned in an exercise book on the kitchen table while all the children milled around. So urgent was the need, it couldn't wait! The book was illustrated with Norman's pictures and published in both Britain and Australia.

By the time the third doctor came to take his turn at the clinic, over three thousand patients had been treated, and still they came. The doctors were always hard-pressed, and Norman continued to learn many useful things under their guidance as he lent a hand. In the interests of public health, one of the medics isolated a scabies bug and put it under a microscope on display. It looked very fierce and many fascinated folk queued up to view this wonder! It represented one of many efforts to give simple instruction on health and hygiene. But such endeavours were an uphill battle against overwhelming ignorance and superstition.

For instance, it was believed that head lice came with rain drops, so be careful not to get rain on your hair! As for washing your hair, it was not only foolish but actually dangerous! Because of various taboos and practices governing pregnancy and childbirth, mothers suffered malnutrition and often got infections and blood poisoning.

Apart from the oppression of spiritual darkness and superstition, the Hualong team was conscious of increasing political pressure. Financially, conditions were going from bad to worse. Money sent to the missionaries was only about half its value when received. It was perilously easy to look into the uncertain future and allow fear of what might happen tomorrow paralyze what could be done today. "We're thankful," they wrote to Mother Lascelles, "to have an open door to preach Christ, and if we can't do *that*, there is no point in staying."

To help make ends meet, Norman experimented with a garden and was delighted to find that cabbages and carrots did well. Tomatoes never ripened outside, though many green ones were carefully wrapped in newspaper and coaxed to ripen in a dark drawer. One or more pigs (dead!) were cured and later smoked in a small smoke-house.

The missionaries had, perforce, to make everything they needed, literally from scratch. Amy studied the nutritional content of the local raw food stuffs and sought to maintain a balanced diet for the family.

After many months came the welcome news that the long-awaited jeep had reached Lanzhou, and so Norman went down to get it. In the lovely planning of the Lord, they received word at the same time that we two school girls would be coming home for the Christmas holidays.

Dad picked us up from the airfield at Lanzhou and Rupert Clarke from the BMH, and we set off triumphantly for Hualong in the new vehicle. It made such a row, we nicknamed it "Boanerges" (son of thunder).

It was an eventful journey. Halfway home, the fuel pump broke. The jeep was pushed to the nearest hamlet where we were very fortunate to find somewhere to stay overnight. Even better in that perishing cold, there was a warm *kang* on which to sleep. This mud brick bed, large enough to accommodate us all, was heated inside by a smouldering fire of dried animal dung.

Dad and Rupert tinkered about with the engine for a few hours next morning and finally discovered that the jeep could be made to go if Rupert travelled standing up behind Dad, balancing a can of petrol on the roof. The gas, drawn by gravity through rubber tubes (borrowed from the medical kit!), would keep the engine fuelled.

Cautiously, we resumed our journey. We had put on

every bit of warm clothing we could find and were well rugged up but, with the canvas hood rolled back, it was very cold, especially for Rupert. We hoped to make Hwalong before nightfall, but dark had already fallen when, in an attempt to cross a frozen stream, the jeep crashed through thin ice into fairly deep water. By the time help was found to haul us out, it was the middle of the night. A warm welcome awaited us, however. Mother, very anxious about our whereabouts, was still up keeping the fire stoked and a pot of soup simmering on the hob. Rapturously we fell into each others' arms. It was marvellous to be home and together again.

"Boanerges" was, unfortunately, out of action for a long time, until spare parts could be obtained. But after that, the shuttling of medical personnel continued more efficiently and life was made considerably easier for the team.

Christmas 1948 was memorable because, although none of us realized it, this was the last Christmas the family would have together for four years. We older children wouldn't see Dad again for more than three years. It was as well the future was hidden from us or it would have cast a dark shadow over this most joyous festival.

Mother had us all busily making presents and Christmas goodies. She taught me to use the hand-machine and I proudly sewed a frilly apron for her out of material that had been wrapped around a food parcel. She could always create something out of nothing. I remember the magnificent Red Indian outfit she made Alastair from food parcel wrappings, feathers from various fowls and scraps of coloured wool. On the great day, Father Christmas himself arrived in full regalia, his costume contrived out of red blankets and cotton wool, and was hailed a howling success.

Mother opened a present from New Zealand and was stunned to unfold her first pair of nylons. Could these filmy things be stockings? Ruefully she surveyed her feet, clad in their thick hose and handmade, wadded shoes. The temperature outside was many degrees below zero. Nylons belonged to another existence!

All too soon, the holidays ended and it was time for us older children to return to Chefoo. Alastair, nearly six, was to go for the first time. Without really understanding what was going on, we youngsters had absorbed something of the increasing tension over the political situation. I, an inveterate worrier like my father, started having nightmares about "wicked men" and would cling frantically to Mother and Dad pleading to be allowed to stay home.

Averil, being like Mother of a more buoyant disposition, had a wonderful dream about God protecting His children. This made a great impression on her and also comforted me. It was a great reassurance to Mother and Dad to realize afresh that the Lord Himself could have personal dealings with their children and would meet our emotional needs.

In Lanzhou there was an interminable wait for a plane. With twelve children, their parents and the teacher-escort, all crammed into inadequate quarters, it was difficult to keep everyone happily occupied and at the same time in a state of permanent readiness for departure should a plane stop by. Week after week we waited, looking expectantly for the Lord to provide.

We were very excited when, at last, a freight plane turned up. It was carrying a load of wool, but the pilot agreed to take the party to Jiujiang. Bundled up against the biting cold, we children were strapped into the bucket seats. The doors were closed and the engines warming up, when an official came running across the tarmac. "Get out everyone. You can't go. The airfield at Jiujiang is flooded."

Unbelievingly, we all watched "our" plane go off without us. It had climbed only a few hundred feet into the air when an engine burst into flames and the aircraft crashed! Back at our quarters again, we joined together to praise God for our marvellous deliverance.

Eventually we did get away in another freight plane. At our feet, strapped to a stretcher, lay the seriously injured pilot of the crashed plane who had been treated at the BMH.

As Norman and Amy watched the fragile little aircraft disappear into the distance, hot tears stung their eyes and pain filled their hearts. These partings never got any easier. Letters were a poor substitute, and even these soon stopped coming as commercial air service to the northwest was suspended. There was no mail for a very long time. The silence was even harder to bear than the separation.

Back in Hualong, however, there were encouragements. The ministry was having more spiritual impact and a number of priests showed definite interest. After the Chinese service on Sundays, Norman and Amy struggled through a service in Tibetan which might be attended by as many as twenty patients. It really stretched them, but they felt they must use every opportunity to tell people of Christ, however inadequate their efforts.

There was more good news. Reinforcements for the Tibetan work had arrived at Xining, the centre for the Tibetan advance. They were Mary Milner from New Zealand and Gertrud Koeppel from Switzerland. Soon after that, George and Dorothy Bell also arrived back in the northwest after five years in their homeland of Canada. They had been, for many years, among CIM's pioneers on the Tibetan border and three of their children were buried in the Gui-de area. Their experience would be a tremendous strength to the team.

The hearts of the Tibetan workers were further cheered by the news that the Tibetan Bible had been published in India, for the first time in history, after ninety years of hard toil. The missionaries longed to hold a copy of this precious book in their hands.

The clinic in Hualong was now well established. Thousands of Tibetans were coming in for treatment. But Norman and Amy felt continually burdened for the countless nomads out on the grasslands who had never heard the gospel message. *We need to go out to them*, they thought. *But how?*

The original plan had been for the McIntoshes to establish a clinic at Hualong and then go on and do the same at Gui-de.

But, by this time, it was becoming clear that, due to the Communist advance and lack of medical personnel, a repetition of the plan at Gui-de would no longer be possible. The border team met to seek the Lord's guidance. To prayer partners Norman wrote:

"You will realize that big decisions are before us, and the way is going to be different from anything previously. Do pray for us, that the Lord will open the way, step by step, and that we shall know the mind of the Lord."

Finally, it was decided that the Macs would live with the Bells at Gui-de and work out to the grasslands from there, doing what medical work they could with the help of a Chinese couple from the BMH who were trained nurses. It was hard to leave the more established work at Hualong to return to raw pioneering again. But the call of the Lord to the nomads was incessant in their hearts.

CHAPTER 9

THE GATES SWING OPEN

As Norman and Amy set off for Gui-de they were acutely aware of the political storm clouds gathering on the horizon. The atmosphere was tense, menacing. How long would they have before the storm broke?

"Be realistic," insinuated the Tempter, "you know it can't be long. What's the use of starting new work at this stage? You won't do any good. The wise thing would be to get out now, while you still can!"

Then came the strengthening word of the Lord to their fearful hearts. "Whoever watches the wind will not plant; whoever looks at the clouds will not reap. As you do not know the path of the wind . . . so you cannot understand the work of God . . . sow your seed in the morning, and at evening let not your hands be idle . . ." (Ecclesiastes 11:5-6).

"Lord," they responded gratefully, "however long or short our day of opportunity in Gui-de may be, we will sow the seed. Help us to keep our eyes off the weather and on You, the Eternal One."

To reach Gui-de they had first to go to Xining where they stopped for a week at the mission station. It was good to spend time with Mary Milner, whom they'd known since childhood, and to get to know Gertrud Koeppel. These two would shortly be joining them at Gui-de which was another three days' journey further into the northwest.

The road to Gui-de crossed a mountain over 13,000 feet high. It was bare, rugged country. On every vantage point, prayer flags fluttered. At certain places there were huge piles of stones, often situated in otherwise stoneless loess areas. Superstitious travellers would carry rocks for miles to throw on these cairns to ensure safety as they journeyed through. Brushwood was packed into what looked like great windbreaks at key mountain passes. These were to entangle malignant spirits and to prevent their passing over from one valley to the next. Norman and Amy were impressed once again by these mute symbols of spiritual bondage.

In a wayside idol house, a woman was prostrating herself before the idols. There were deep polished grooves in the thick wooden floor, depressions worn by the bodies of countless prostrating pilgrims. The woman had small pads for her hands to shoot forward on. Even the ten toe marks were hollowed into the boards. Those kowtowing were supposed to do 108 prostrations each time without stopping, and the exhaustion which followed was indescribable. It hurt even to witness it.

When the Macs made this first trip to Gui-de there had been heavy rain and the roads were hazardous. At one place the jeep bogged down and it took three hours, nine horses and many silver dollars to clear it.

The town came into sight when they were on the opposite side of the wide river. The only way to cross was to drive over a wobbly bridge made of small boats lashed together — not much wider than the vehicle. Amy, ever prone to motion-sickness, almost had to take a Dramamine just to watch it! But soon they were over and safely at their new home.

Gui-de, a small border town near a large bend in the Yellow River, was a busy trading post. Chinese and Muslim merchants ran the town businesses. Outside the settlement, in fields and on the river bank, large caravans of yak were tethered at the end of their long trips from Lhasa and other parts of Central Asia.

Nearby was the mission compound, somewhat isolated. Camel trains passed the door. The camels usually moved in single file, five at a time, roped together. The cameleer sat on the first animal, and a bell was tied to the last. If the bell stopped tinkling while the train plodded its way over dreary miles, the cameleer would know the rope had snapped, and would then turn back to find the animal which had broken loose.

As the camels passed in front of the mission house, quite a quantity of their hair brushed off on to the bushes. This was collected by the local women, spun on a distaff into fine yarn and knitted into warm, hard-wearing garments.

Both yak and camels were laden with heavy bricks of pressed tea, packs of salt, bolts of brocade and other valuables. From Gui-de roads ran in a number of directions right out past the sedentary Tibetan villages into nomad territory.

At 8,000 feet, it was milder than Hualong and, with mountains all around, could actually be very hot during the brief weeks of summer. Then food had to be gathered for the eight to nine months of cold weather. The days were already chilly when the Macs arrived, so they had to get busy immediately laying in winter provisions. Cabbages were stacked up outside to freeze. Potatoes, carrots, onions and eggs were stored in deep pits underground.

For many months there were no letters from the children at school. In the South, the Communists were "liberating" one area after another. What was happening in Jiangsu? Were the children safe?

Then one bleak day, came definite news. The Chefoo School at Guling was now under Communist control. Pale and silent, Norman and Amy went about their work, their hearts full of unanswered questions. Their only anchor was trust in God. "You, not the Communists, are in control of our children. We commit them once again into Your safe keeping." When mails resumed later, a letter from an understanding friend in New Zealand assured them that, in regard to the children, "He is able to keep that which we have committed to Him" (2 Timothy 1:12).

By this time, the Gui-de area had become a kind of

political no man's land. When the last of the regular army left, lawlessness prevailed. Old scores were paid off, looting was rife, and the Macs lived in daily expectation that even their unpretentious home would be ransacked. They tried to prepare a few necessities in case this happened. The strain of it all, however, proved too much, causing Amy to have a miscarriage at four-and-a-half months. The sadness remained for a long time, even though she knew in her heart the peace which passes understanding. Later, she realized that God, in His mercy, had allowed this to happen. If she had carried the baby to full term, she would probably have needed surgery and there would have been no doctor or medical help available.

Lacking reliable news, rumours abounded. But clearly, the Liberation Army was drawing nearer. Finally, one Sunday afternoon, it arrived. No one knew what to expect. With a few church friends, the McIntoshes stood outside the front gate and watched some seven hundred men in full battle dress, with fixed bayonets, march singing towards the town ahead. *What is this going to mean?* they thought anxiously. As if in an audible voice, came the words of Psalm 139, "The darkness and the light are both alike to Thee." Whatever the future held, God would be with them, strong and unchanging.

The next day, a posse of military men came and "borrowed" the radio which had kept them in touch with the outside world. And that was that. But other than that, life went on more or less normally for many months.

At long last, mail again filtered through from Chefoo, the first tangible link with the children for five months. How Norman and Amy read and re-read those letters! Amy wrote to her mother "The children are very happy at school. It is lovely to see their work improving and themselves developing. The staff is simply wonderful! Such loving, intimate notes on the various letters, and such watchful care of every child. I really think Chefoo School must be unique in this world!"

They hoped they'd be able to see Chefoo for themselves. It would soon be time for Gavin to go to school, but with changing conditions, would this be possible? They could only pray and wait to see what God would do.

Through the months they had been in Gui-de Norman had established a small clinic and was receiving many calls for medical help. In that wild border country, he was often required to attend to bullet wounds. One day, a little Muslim girl of eleven years was carried in. She had just had her right hand blown off while playing with a hand grenade. It was a gory mess with only the little finger still intact. Norman had to clip off the thumb bone with a pair of pliers. There was no proper anaesthetic, only morphine, but the brave child made never a whimper through the whole nasty business. Thereafter, Mary went to dress the hand until it was healed.

Gradually, Norman, onetime carpenter and shepherd, became known throughout the area as Arka Mamba (Uncle Doctor). His medical skills secured for him what hitherto had been denied foreigners — entrance into the Tibetan villages, unhindered travel across the grasslands, open doors into the homes and lamaseries and everywhere ready ears for the gospel. It was incredible that, after all these years of waiting, the rusty hinges to the nomads were swinging wide so quickly. These naturally suspicious and elusive people were actually sending invitations to the foreigners!

A large deputation came to ask Norman to go and pull teeth for an important Living Buddha who was then about fifty miles away on the grasslands. This meant a hard ride through territory infested with brigands, but at each particularly dangerous place, armed fellow-travellers appeared to escort the Lord's servant through.

Later, Norman found out that in one narrow valley, five armed brigands lying in ambush had remained hidden when they saw the man who was accompanying him. This fellow was renowned as a crack-shot throughout the grasslands.

Finally, they arrived at a high valley where there were sixteen yak-hair tents, low and black against the grazing grounds. Vicious dogs leaped out at their approach, snapping and snarling but, at a shout from one of the men, women and children raced out of the tents and threw themselves on the dogs to hold them down. Then Norman was led to the Rimpoche, the Precious One, the Living Buddha.

He was an old man, and the stethoscope revealed that his heart was in bad shape. Norman was afraid to extract the requested five teeth all at once in that altitude, so decided to pull one first and see how the patient stood up to it.

That night, alone in his tent, the Arka Mamba tossed and turned on his bed of felts. Visions of what could happen to him if the old man died while under treatment passed through his mind. He felt very vulnerable. "Lord," he cried, "deliver me from fear and enable me to trust You."

Next morning, however, all was well, so he went ahead and extracted the other teeth. While the simple operation was going on in the tent, the priests outside were blowing their horns and chanting, a lot of noise being necessary to protect their Rimpoche.

As Norman was preparing to leave, his important patient invited him to stay on a day or two longer to see a gathering of Tibetans from far and near. They were coming to bring their annual gifts to the Living Buddha. It was a unique experience for a westerner.

The Living Buddha, enthroned on a great pile of sheepskins, with great formality received scores of his subjects. They brought bolts of beautiful brocade (from India), large shoes of silver, bladders of yak butter, and many other valuable offerings which were piled high around him. As each devotee stepped forward and proffered his gift, the Living Buddha presented him with a tiny packet of black sugar or the like and followed this with a puff of his "holy" breath.

Every summer this "god" left his lamasery to travel around the grasslands collecting dues from the nomads. It seemed to Norman that he was just robbing his people of their wealth and giving nothing in return.

The whole pageant impressed him deeply. The remembrance of it inspired a sermon that he often preached. I Samuel 8:10-18 warns how the king of this world will treat his subjects. "He will take . . . He will take . . . He will take. . ." How different from our Precious One. "He who did not spare his own son but gave him up for us all, will he not also with him graciously give us all things?" (Romans 8:32)

George worked around the Gui-de area, mostly among the sedentary Tibetans while Norman took extensive tours out into the grasslands, usually staying away about two weeks at a time. Occasionally Amy and the children would accompany him.

Previously, when in China, they had worn Chinese dress. Now they wore sheepskin gowns in the cold weather and wadded shoes and boots with thick soles. Norman wore a red fox fur hat and heavy leather thigh boots when on long trips and, except that he was minus a gun, looked indistinguishable from other Tibetan horsemen. Instead of a weapon, he toted a camera. Along with his medicine, he invariably carried plenty of literature in Tibetan, Chinese and Arabic. While the common people were illiterate, the priests could read and they were ubiquitous in that society.

Among the few personal belongings he took on these trips, Norman always included his well-worn copy of *The Golden Treasury of English Verse*. He loved poetry and, as he jogged along through the Tibetan mountains on horse or mule, he would read favourite pieces out aloud or quote from the poet so dear to his Scottish heart. The shy marmots would remind him of Burns' lines to a field mouse, "Wee sleekit, cow'rin, tim'rous beastie." But here all likeness ceased. The hedgerows and nightingales of The Green Isles were a far cry from the bleak loneliness through which he travelled!

Norman always had trouble finding reliable mounts for these treks. Finally, a lively mule had thrown him when a faulty bit broke in its mouth. He damaged several ribs which were extremely painful. As he groaned around the house, Amy teased, "Do you think Adam felt like this? Perhaps you're going to have another wife!"

"One is more than enough!" he retorted. "But seriously, I think the time has come to get a good horse of our own. Let's ask the Lord to provide one."

God answered that prayer in a very lovely manner. Far away at Chefoo School, staff and students were looking for a practical project to which they could give their "Lord's portion." They decided to save up and send Mr McIntosh the money to buy a horse for visiting the nomads. They also decreed that the horse's name should be "Bao Shee" (Spreader of Good News). In due time, a photograph of Norman in full Tibetan costume, astride Bao Shee, was displayed on the notice board at Chefoo, to the delight of the donors. This sturdy mount was a great boon for the many outstation trips, and much more reliable than hired beasts.

In one sedentary Tibetan village, the Macs were given a sheep as payment for services rendered. This they tethered, but shortly afterwards a boy came running to say that, unfortunately, the sheep had killed itself. As Buddhists, the villagers would not take life, but so arranged the tether rope that, when given a fright, the sheep would rush forward and strangle itself. So the people got all the meat they wanted!

While all this ministry went on largely unhindered by the authorities, the Communists were, nevertheless, gradually strengthening their grip on the people. Although nobody realized it, their influence had already penetrated the mission station. The mission cook and househelp was a Christian man called Brother Iron. About this time, he and his wife began to receive a visitor who spent hours with them, almost daily. Unknown to himself or to those for whom he worked, Brother Iron was having his thinking changed, the results of which would all too soon become evident.

The question of Gavin getting to school was becoming more pressing. He badly needed the companionship and stimulus of children his own age. One morning, as Norman and Amy were praying about it, the Lord spoke quite definitely in their minds, "Go to the authorities immediately and apply for a travel pass to Guling."

Humanly speaking, it was most unlikely that such permission would be granted, but they did as they were told. Believing that this was of God, Amy put in a concentrated week or two sewing Gavin's outfit. She sang as she worked and mentally planned their trip. They hadn't had a holiday for three years. Then she noticed that Norman was rather quiet.

"What's the matter, Norm?" she asked. "Don't you believe we're going?"

"It's not that," he replied slowly. "I hate to say it, but I don't think I can go with you to Guling."

"Why ever not?" she asked in dismay.

"I just sense that we are not going to have much longer to preach the gospel here. It tears me in two, but I believe I must stay and use every possible moment among the Tibetans. Can you manage the trip on your own?"

"I suppose I'll have to," was the sober response, "but you know I'd sooner walk barefoot through a paddock of hedgehogs!"

Was this the Lord's will? Norman and Amy had never sacrificed "the children" for "the work." Both were sacred trusts from the Lord. Both were equally important. When an apparent clash occurred, they sought the Lord for guidance and trusted Him with the outcome. As they prayed now, the Lord confirmed that, in this case, the ministry to the Tibetans had to come before the needs of the family.

This decision was no sooner reached than the passes were granted. It was July 1950.

Norman escorted Amy and the children to Xining where, delightful surprise, they were joined by the Preedy family who had also been granted passes. No return permission was given and it was a case of trusting the Lord that this would be granted in Guling when needed. On the trip over from Gui-de Twinkle's mule gave a sudden jolt and tossed her into a shallow stream. What they thought was a sprained wrist was shown later, under the Chefoo fluoroscope, to be a greenstick fracture which had healed.

Norman returned to Gui-de alone and wrote to Mother Lascelles, "The house is like a grave without Gavin and Twinkle dashing about. It is dreadful coming home from a call out to sick folks to have no sunny little fellow waiting at the gate with his loving welcome. But it is no good dwelling on that, and the heartaches we can only commit to the Lord for His healing touch."

Meanwhile the travellers were having an eventful journey. Later Amy described it to her mother, "Our being here in Guling is a miracle. No one near here is allowed a pass, yet we from Tibet have got through. The trip from Xining to Lanzhou took fourteen-and-a-half hours! We arrived dehydrated and too tired to eat. Then four days to Xian — in a bus with iron bars along the sides and one door that opened from the outside.

"We had a marvellous deliverance on the last day when gasoline ignited on the driver's seat. It was a close shave for us all. I was able to give first-aid to the mechanic whose hand was badly burnt. He'd lost his hair and eyebrows too. He was terribly grateful. Turned out to be a Christian and on his first trip from Lanzhou.

"Went by train from Xian to Zhengzhou and arrived twenty-two hours later. A China Travel Service man met us and took us to a nice hotel where we washed, ate and rested for the next six hours. At nine o'clock we boarded the Beijing-Hankou express with its good sleepers and good meals. I wrote Norman that we were having a lovely time, just to keep his cheque book handy!

"At Hankou we had three days' wait, finally getting on a large river steamer which did the trip to Jiujiang in ten hours. We got fifth class(!) the boat being full before we applied. Sat out all night on the deck with no covering except fresh air, the moon and a blanket! Had lunch with our folk at Jiujiang, and set off by truck to the foot of the hill. There we got sedan chairs, and in two-and-a-half hours were carried to the top.

"You can imagine how we felt as we got nearer and nearer the Promised Land. Just as we got out of the chairs at the top, along came May Conway with all the kiddies. Then you should have seen the flying arms and legs. They all looked so bonny!"

At Guling, we McIntoshes were given our own cottage on the holiday compound, "Fairy Glen," and had our own table at the communal meals. It was the nearest thing to home, except that we missed Dad so much.

No time length had been given for Mother's stay in Guling. Word came from the local authorities that she could not return to Qinghai unless the officials there granted permission. So it was a day-to-day life filled with good things, hikes, picnics, fun and fellowship.

Mother and Clarence Preedy also organized a special mission for the Chefoo children. It was the highlight of the summer. A number of children gave their lives to the Saviour. One girl wrote, "I wept in the meeting this morning when I thought that for nine years I have lived my life without Christ." She later became a prominent gospel singer in her homeland. Another girl, the same age, also came to Christ and is a leader today in the educational world of her home country. A six-year-old boy, whose mother was also spending time at Chefoo, said to her one night at bedtime (after a meeting), "Mummy, I want to give my heart to Jesus — *now*!" A few months later this little lad was killed instantly in a cycling accident.

Then suddenly, after five happy weeks, Amy and Twinkle were ordered to leave for the northwest the following day. As Amy packed her cases that night her heart felt like lead. It was desperately hard to say goodbye again, this time to four of her children.

Next morning, we four waved until her sedan chair vanished from sight down the mountainside. To her, looking back, we seemed so small and vulnerable standing there. Her heart ached with sadness. Then, in rhythm with the coolies' tramping feet, came the comforting refrain, "Peace, perfect peace, with loved ones far away? In Jesus' keeping we are safe — and they."

The journey back from Chefoo took a whole month! All went well, till the stage by bus from Xian. One night, the driver gambled away the hours, and the next day went to sleep at the wheel. The bus ran off the road and toppled into a ditch. Amy thought her nose was broken and it was seven days before they got to BMH and the X-ray. Fortunately however, only the cartilage was dislocated, but her looks were greatly enhanced by a beautiful black eye. They thanked the Lord for His protection in what could have been a nasty accident. Then it was on to Xining to find Norman waiting to escort them on the final leg of the journey to Gui-de It was so good to be together again.

During Amy's absence, Norman had spent an extremely busy three months. Every day brought further confirmation that he had done the right thing by staying behind. Medical and preaching opportunities continued to abound.

One husky young Tibetan was so grateful that Norman had been able to heal his baby son of congenital syphilis, that he swore to be a blood brother. An unarmed traveller was simply asking for a bullet as he rode past hidden snipers, and this man felt responsible for the safety of his unarmed "brother." Many times he accompanied Norman across dangerous grasslands and always carried his gun with its two-pronged stand in a conspicuous way for all to see. The young fellow was really sincere, according to the light he had, and eagerly listened as Norman explained to him about the Lord Jesus, the Living Word and Saviour of the world.

While Amy had been in Guling, Norman had received a cable from London to say that her second book *Daughter of Tibet* was about to be published and would he send photographs? Also a filmstrip was being made of *The Man in the Sheepskin*. This was heartening news to come home to.

The greatest news of all, however, was that George Bell had baptized seven people, including two Tibetan women! These were the first fruits after twenty years of labour in that area. It seemed that a lama also was close to believing. He had apparently already left the lamasery and had come to church without his priestly robes.

Even as they rejoiced at this breakthrough, the general situation became more threatening. The sky was now black with clouds. Some missionaries had decided to leave, which was unsettling for those who remained. In a letter, Norman expressed his feelings.

"From now on, I gather, there will be a thinning of the ranks. My own thoughts on this matter? I know what the natural man would like to do, and he wouldn't take ten minutes to do it either. But there is a higher will that directs our paths, and we do so long to remain always in the will of the Lord. The only thing that makes me question our stand in any way is the effect our presence is having, or will yet have, on the local church. But God has always clearly directed us hitherto, and we have this confidence, that should He ask any further step, the way will be made unmistakable."

Supporters in the homelands, however, were growing concerned for their safety. A letter came from Jack and Lois Morrison in Geraldine, New Zealand. "The Lord has prompted us to write and offer to take your children if it should ever be necessary for them to leave China without you. We would take every responsibility for them and care for them as our own."

Norman and Amy were touched by the love and concern that motivated this offer but were quite decided in their own minds that, if it should ever come to that, they would leave the country with their children.

This decision was very soon to be taken out of their hands!

To Amy's increasingly anxious mother they wrote, "The Lord has never recalled His commission to us, and we have never regretted obeying Him. The night is certainly getting darker. Do not pray any soft things for us at this time, for we need courage, and calmness and a sound mind."

One morning, Amy stepped out of the door and there, a few feet away, was a magnificent golden-headed eagle, standing about three feet high. They stared at each other in amazement for several minutes until the eagle flew off. She had no idea why it was there, or where it had come from. But it was superb in flight as it headed towards the snow-caps that pierced the blue Qinghai sky. The unusual encounter was a timely reminder from God that "Those who hope in the Lord will renew their strength. They will soar on wings like eagles; they will run and not grow weary, they will walk and not be faint" (Isaiah 40:31).

Surprisingly, at this time, the Bells were granted passes to go to Guling, and had been gone only one month when the storm finally broke over the heads of the Gui-de contingent. George Bell was falsely accused of many crimes, the ugliest being that he had sexually assaulted the cook's wife.

CHAPTER 10

THROUGH DEEP WATERS

T he fury of hate that was now unleashed upon them left them gasping. Not only George, but Norman also was accused of serious crimes. He was spying for America. He had robbed the people. He had caused the death of many patients.

Who was the informer who had laid these false charges against them?

Brother Iron. Oh, no! Their trusted friend. Now they realized what the propagandists had been doing to him, how his mind had been manipulated and truth distorted until it was possible for this Christian man to do so fearful a thing.

They felt as though they had been kicked in the stomach. In all their missionary career, this was the worst thing that had ever happened to them. They moved about the house in a state of shock, physically ill and even sicker in spirit. Now they understood more intimately how their Lord had felt when Judas, His close companion and friend, had betrayed Him. History was repeating itself and they were entering into a deeper experience of the fellowship of His sufferings, a bitter cup indeed.

There was terrible pain in their hearts for Brother Iron and the whole affair. They discovered later that this pattern was being systematically followed throughout the land — a discrediting of God's servants by those nearest to them. Norman and Amy sent out an SOS for prayer: "Get our friends praying, will you? So often, the devil attacks at

Christmas when so many folk are preoccupied at home with other things. It is when they take a holiday from prayer that we know it here!"

Then the church deacons paid a surreptitious visit. "Please don't meet with us again," they requested.

It was not unexpected, in fact it was quite understandable. But the reality of it left Norman and Amy desolate, as Jesus felt when His disciples all deserted Him and fled. The reign of terror was upon them too. Who could blame them?

The issue was intentionally confused. It was not to the Communist interests in those early days to persecute people just because they were Christians. That would only have stimulated a spirit of martyrdom. No, the missionaries were to be rejected as foreign imperialists, condemned for criminal activities and hated as enemies of the people.

The church also was under scrutiny and Chinese Christians were likely to be accused of being "running dogs of the foreigner." Before long, recrimination meetings were being conducted among national believers as well. Then brother was incited to rise up against brother. All over China the same story was being repeated and the church lay torn and bleeding.

It was obvious that the presence of the missionaries at Gui-de, as elsewhere, was now an embarrassment to the very people they had come to serve. Their ministry was over. They had to go. Their hearts were full of grief when they thought of the unfinished work amongst the Tibetans. It was like a bereavement.

Just before the storm broke at Gui-de, a directive had come from headquarters. The entire CIM was to withdraw from China! It seemed unbelievable that a mission which had hung on tenaciously through almost a century of political and social upheaval should now have to leave so ignominiously. Was this to be the end of the China Inland Mission as well?

On Christmas Eve, the mail runner arrived, after his three-day run from Xining, carrying a telegram which required an immediate answer. Headquarters inquired what

Norman and Amy wanted done with their four children in the event of the school having to be disbanded before the parents got their exit passes. As there was no telegraph office at Gui-de, the runner, after resting an hour, would set out on the return journey to Xining.

"Before they call, I will answer," the Lord has promised. (Isaiah 65:24) He had prepared for this emergency months before when Jack and Lois Morrison had known God calling them to offer a home for the children. So now, Norman and Amy just looked at each other wordlessly. Norman reached for a pen and wrote the Morrison's address on the telegraph form. Everything just fitted into place. They knew this was of the Lord, and the knowledge brought great peace and comfort. Naturally, they still hoped it would be possible to meet up with the family en route, and all go to New Zealand together. But God, in His mercy, hid the future.

They set about making application for exit visas, and sold (for a mere trifle) most of their few possessions in preparation for departure. Even this sorrowful task had its lighter moments.

Their teacher, a Tibetan sorcerer, whose hair when unwound reached the ground, selected Amy's old maternity skirt and a swim suit. Whatever was that doing in Tibetan country? Probably, he valued the woollen material in both.

Funny the things missionaries hang on to. Gertrud, who had been a ballet-dancer before her conversion, had brought along with her a magnificent full-length evening dress, made of exquisite organdy medallions. The Macs don't know who collected that bargain!

Then, with practically nothing left, they awaited permission to leave.

At this point, they were put under house arrest. Their bank account was frozen and their mail passed to the military by the post office. Outgoing mail also had to be handed in to the police. Norman was allowed into the town only to get mail and money (a small amount, never enough, allotted to them each week from their account) and to purchase food and fuel.

He was not permitted to converse with anyone and out of consideration for others, did not try to do so. However, kindly shopkeepers passed on significant news in whispers as they served him.

Then the interrogations began.

Because George and Dorothy did not return to Gui-de, the brunt of the inquisition fell on Norman. The authorities went from house to house through the district trying to get accusations against George, but not one person spoke against him. He had lived twenty years in this area and knew many of the people as well as his own family. They were loyal under great pressure, which showed Christian Brother Iron in an even worse light. Because of the attitude of the public, the authorities were furious and vented their spleen on Norman.

He was called up for questioning, day after day, sometimes for as long as eight hours at a stretch. Questions and cross-questions, insults and curses, were hurled at him by three or four examiners at once, in an effort to trap him into contradictions and self-accusations. Fatigue and fear would threaten to cloud his mind and he prayed over and over, "Lord, help me to remember what I've said. Don't let me contradict myself."

He became aware that his interrogators were afraid of one another, each one knowing that his performance would be reported on by the others. Fear and distrust were at every level of society. The officer in charge was the most venomous. He had been educated in a liberal Christian university and had thereby been robbed of his old beliefs without finding a satisfying substitute or a living Saviour. This man's hatred for Christ was so great that he would yell and scream with anger until he frothed at the mouth.

These men surrounded Norman like ravening wolves. They threatened him with prison, concentration camp and even expulsion to the Siberian salt mines. Sometimes he felt himself sinking in the fearful mire of lies. Everything became confused. What was true and what was false?

Back home afterwards, he would shake for hours with

nervous reaction until gradually the peace of God took over and he knew again the security of the everlasting arms underneath him. The strong, loving companionship of Amy and the others on these occasions helped to keep him from losing his grip. In fact, the strain under which they all lived, bound them very close together and drew forth deep mutual support as they encouraged one another to trust in the faithfulness of God.

Gertrud, being Swiss, was granted a visa early on. She felt it very keenly going off on the long journey to the coast and leaving her fellow-workers behind.

The Macs and Mary were left to sit out the winter together. It was hard not to become discouraged as the long, icy weeks dragged by. The terrible tension that had gripped them at first gradually subsided, then boredom became their greatest enemy. Further pressure came as they heard of fellow-missionaries in trouble. Rupert Clarke, in Hualong, was being charged with murder.

With the coming of the birds and new green to the bare trees, however, hope sprang afresh in their hearts. Surely, very soon now they would be allowed to leave.

Being away from the town, they could take short walks without drawing attention to themselves, though they were conscious of always being under surveillance. These outings brought great relief and healing. Now that they had more time to observe things, they found themselves appreciating the beauties of nature in a new way. On one outing, they were uplifted to see a large, white goose on one of the tributaries of the Yellow River nearby, probably migrating elsewhere. A symbol of freedom! Like children they played and tossed stones into the water.

Through the long, weary days, they often talked about things in the homeland. Where would they set up house after so many years in the East? It was a great comfort to have Twinkle with them. She was almost five years old and a cheery little companion. When they told her about taps, she was very worried about going to New Zealand. How would she ever know which was the hot or cold tap when she got to Nana's house?

Concerning the pleasure the child was to them, Amy wrote her mother, "About six in the morning, when Norman gets up to make tea, Twinkle's out of bed, into her Chinese gown and slippers, and away to the kitchen with him, talking all the while like a gramophone. She loves to get him going on an argument, something different every morning. For instance, she says with a coy look, 'You like little girls, don't you?' 'No!' roars Dad, 'I like little boys!' Twinkle fairly purrs, she has got him started! Or maybe, with a smile, 'You like Betsy Ann (her doll) don't you?' 'No!' roars Dad, 'why should I?' and proceeds to say a lot of defamatory things about said doll. Twinkle's repartee is delightful, and it's very funny listening in."

By May 1951 we older children had been evacuated from China and had arrived safely in Geraldine. Although Mother and Dad kept writing, many of their letters never got through. Under the circumstances, it was amazing that so much mail did reach its destination. They were especially touched to receive a note from J O Sanders. He had visited us in Geraldine and then, with his usual thoughtfulness, had furnished them with the details for which he knew they'd be hungering.

The three adults disciplined themselves to fill the empty days as creatively as possible and so forestall the creeping inertia and depression that results from boredom. They took to re-reading Dickens. They invented word games and became expert Lexicon players. On Sundays, they organized a stiff Bible quiz, prepared by each in turn, aimed to show up the ignorance of the others! They made their own fun, especially when celebrations came around.

On Amy's birthday, she found a cake of soap in a scrap of pretty paper, "with love from Norman." He was a good soap maker but this time, due to lack of proper ingredients, the whole batch looked as though it had been struck by lightning. Somehow Mary managed to scratch together a fairly presentable birthday cake. So, teasing and joking, they forced themselves to turn this and similar occasions into cheerful celebrations that helped keep the black beast of fear at bay.

As always, though, the most solid comfort came from the Lord through their meditative study of His Word. They had more time for this now. Even so, this took discipline and determination as boredom and worry so easily undermined concentration. Norman was working through Genesis with the aid of Griffith Thomas and finding the story of Joseph especially applicable, even to the butler forgetting him! But in the end Joseph could say, "You intended to harm me, but God intended it for good . . ." (Genesis 50:20).

Amy, meanwhile, was in Hosea with Campbell Morgan, being encouraged to see God behind this dark experience they were going through, as He promised, "I will make the Valley of Achor (trouble) a door of hope" (Hosea 2:15).

Of trouble there was plenty. There were daily (and nightly) petty harassments by the police and, from time to time, fresh accusations would result in further interrogations and renewed tension. Their hearts were heavy when they heard that Rupert had been put in prison, but his optimistic note read, "We expect to get a pass just any month now!"

One hot summer night, Norman was stung on the arm by a scorpion while he was asleep. He flung the creature off and it stung his other arm. Eighteen hours of intense pain had to be endured as they had parted with Novocaine and other medicines earlier with the sale of their stuff.

Then he had sprung a hernia. The Macs were rather worried that it might strangulate, so, in an effort to keep the lump in, Amy fished out her old maternity corset and laced him into it. He strutted around the bedroom patting his corseted abdomen and shouting, "Behold a mother in Israel! That's what I am!" They both laughed until they cried, which, while good for the spirit, was probably bad for the hernia, but the makeshift binder did the trick and held things together until he got to surgery in New Zealand.

As the months passed sluggishly by and the exit passes did

not come, they were tempted to fret. It seemed such a waste of life and time just to sit there doing nothing. Through this desert experience however, the Lord gave his children some precious promises. When all else seemed to fail, they were encouraged to hold fast to His unbreakable word.

One of these was Jeremiah 42:11-12: "Do not be afraid of the king of Babylon whom you now fear. Do not be afraid of him, declares the Lord, for I am with you and will save you and deliver you from his hands. I will show you compassion so that he will have compassion on you and restore you to your land."

They were convinced that God had spoken to them personally. Then came the devil. "Has God really given you this promise?" he taunted. "Are you sure this isn't a figment of your imagination, conceived by your own strong desires? This verse wasn't written for you. You will never see New Zealand again!" How they had to resist him by faith, but as they resisted they found their spirits strengthened.

Unlike those Pacific Islanders who, when they were told that the Lord was coming, didn't plant their crops, Norman went ahead and put in the vegetable garden in the spring, though he fully expected they would all have gone long before anything was ready to eat. This fortunate (and biblical!) combination of faith and works meant that they were able to augment their scanty diet with very welcome fresh vegetables that summer.

Occasionally old friends, especially Tibetans, would slip small gifts of food to them. One priest, in particular, would come down, watch to see if any Communist guards were about and then, if the coast was clear, throw over the wall a hunk of dried meat, a bladder packed with butter or a bag of parched barley flour! Such offerings would bring a lump to the throat and warmth to the heart. They were precious beyond measure.

At last, after eight months, came the welcome order to proceed to Xining. Finally they were on the move! *Not long now,* their hearts sang, *perhaps we'll be home for Christmas!*

Clarence Preedy, who was there on his own, was exceedingly glad to see them. Xining, by this time, was the last occupied mission station before the coast, two thousand miles away!

Betty and Arthur Saunders, with baby David, had just gone. They were the last of the Gansu missionaries. The members of Betty's church had set themselves to pray in shifts around the clock till God gave them their request.

Somehow, it was the Qinghai missionaries, the Tibetan border team, who had got left behind in the general exodus. They were the farthest inland and, when they knew that everyone else had gone, felt desperately isolated and vulnerable.

By this time Rupert was all alone in Hualong. They were concerned that there'd been no word from him for a month. Arthur and Wilda Mathews, with their little daughter, Lilah, were still cooped up waiting at their station, a day's journey away in another direction.

At Xining, two months went by and the Macs and company were not given permission to proceed any further. The weather was getting much colder. They had not taken their heaviest clothing to Xining, never for a moment expecting to be detained there into the winter. What were they to do? The total sum of their worldly possessions covered about half a single bed!

They eyed a wool-filled curtain that hung between two doors. Yes, something might be done with that. It was unpicked and the raw wool washed. Then Norman and Mary set to work to teaze it all up fluffy. Out of it Amy made wadded trousers for the two men. Other bits and pieces were used to contrive garments for Mary and Twinkle, and Amy found enough unspun camel's hair to make a wadded jacket for herself. When the Macs had disposed of their belongings so long before, the authorities had been very annoyed about it, and demanded that they get everything back. Out of fear, quite a number of people had returned items, but it was quite impossible to retrieve stuff that had gone into Tibet and further. The money that remained, however, was enough to meet their needs during the months of detention. Norman dug a hole in the floor to hide this private reserve without which they would never have survived. In the providence of God, the supply didn't run dry until the week they left!

The authorities confiscated the goods that were returned and shut them up in a room on the Xining compound. They sealed the door with a long strip of very flimsy rice paper on which was the stamp of officialdom. On no account was the seal to be broken, which meant that none of their personal property could be used.

One day while playing, little Twinkle pushed against this ill-fitting door and broke the seal. Norman and Amy were terrified. This would be regarded as a major felony. Whatever were they to do?

For three hours they paced back and forth, trying to still their churning stomachs, before Norman plucked up enough courage to go to the authorities to confess. He put on a second pair of trousers, for prison could be cold, gave Amy the keys and went off. Sick at heart, she watched him disappear and wondered if she would ever see him again.

So it was a great surprise when, shortly afterwards, he returned in the company of a single official. This was unusual. Generally, the Communist officials operated in pairs, so that the ever-present company of a witness would ensure that orders were carried out by both.

This man came in to inspect the seal. Suddenly, Twinkle, sensing her parents' anxiety, burst into tears. The offical looked at her and at them and came to some decision in his mind. He gave them a tremendous scolding, then resealed the door. "Make sure it doesn't happen again," he threatened, "or you will be in serious trouble!" And that was the end of the matter. It was nothing short of a miracle! Such trifles could fester into ugly situations. With deep gratitude Norman and Amy bowed before their Lord. Surely He had saved them.

A while later a letter arrived from Mother Lascelles, "Were you in any trouble on the morning of . . . ? (The very day of the breaking of the seal.) I woke with a feeling of real oppression for you. It was so great that I locked the back and front doors of the house, so that people would think I was not at home . . . and for *three hours* I cried to the Lord for you. At the end of that time, the burden lifted, and I knew it was all right. What was the trouble?"

Soon after this, Amy wrote to her, "On 1 December, at five minutes to noon, it will be one year since we entered the Valley of Baca (tears). Your prayers have been answered in that we have been able to make many wells while 'passing through.' Not a permanent dwelling place as you will see." (Psalm 84:6)

"The Valley of Achor" and "the Valley of Baca" aptly described the emotional experiences they suffered that long, hard year. Through trouble and tears God's servants had learned to prove Him in a new way. . . literally to count on His faithfulness for their very lives, and in His power to overcome the paralysis of fear; and finally to come to the place of Job, who cried in the dark, "Though He slay me, yet will I trust Him."

Amy came to this point when reading Daniel chapter three. To Nebuchadnezzar those three young men made the bold claim, "Our God *can* deliver us! But if not . . .!" Amy had lived in the very real expectation of being reunited with her children some day. Now God was probing her soul. "But if not? Will you still go on trusting Me, even then?"

"Yes, Lord, even then," she was able to reply, "for if I lose You, I lose everything."

It was in one dark hour when hope had almost flickered out, that the Lord brought Norman to a new and greater dedication to Himself through the words of Zechariah in Luke 1:74-75. "That He would grant unto us, that we being delivered out of the hand of our enemies might serve Him without fear, in holiness and righteousness before Him, *all the days of our life.*"

Arthur Mathews wrote from their station that they were still marching around the walls of their Jericho, which were "going to come a cropper soon!"

The Macs felt increasingly anxious about Rupert. Though he was only two days' travel away from Xining, they'd had no news of him for three months. The last they'd heard was that he was out of prison and living in the mission compound again.

The Xining contingent tried to put their energies into preparing for Christmas once more, in spite of the disappointment of not being home with their families. They hung up a large "Immanuel" on the wall. Its message meant more than ever before to them this year. "We are not alone," they reassured each other, "God is with us!"

Every day the peace and tranquility of the mission compound was shattered by a blaring loudspeaker. One of these had been placed within sound of every home in the city, and endless propaganda came over, and the same songs . . . day after day, week after week.

It was horrifying to hear public trials being conducted close by, and those found "guilty" being taken away and shot. The hearts of the unwilling listeners ached for every person who passed into eternity without Christ.

Then suddenly, just when it seemed that their detention would go on for ever, the Macs and Mary got word to go. On 8 January, 1952, one year and one month after their ordeal began, they started their journey to Hong Kong. They felt terrible to be leaving Clarence on his own again. As it happened, he was not to be released for another year, at which time he came out with Wilda Mathews and Lilah. Arthur Mathews and Rupert Clarke were held for even longer! The story of their detention, with particular reference to how the Lord sustained the Mathews family through suffering, is recorded in *Green Leaf in Drought*, by Isobel Kuhn.

The journey to Canton took eleven days by truck, bus and train. The McIntosh party did not travel under guard but, at each stop, had to report to the police. They'd be frisked and their meagre luggage emptied out and gone through with a fine-tooth comb. Twice, due to breakdowns, they were unable to keep up with the schedule on their travel passes, and were accused of spying. When this happened, dark fear descended. "Oh God," they pleaded, "don't let them send us back now!"

At the border they were kept waiting for hours. Only a barbed wire fence and a few yards of no man's land stood between them and freedom. They could see the Union Jack fluttering in the breeze. So near and yet so far! To their consternation, another westerner was turned back from the very border, and the look on his face was to haunt them for years.

Then they were called. "Hand over any American dollars," demanded a female guard, standing in Amy's way. "Take off your hat!" snapped a Communist soldier to Norman. They were frisked and glared at for the last time. Then, at a grudging nod, they moved over the bridge — to freedom!

Something broke inside them. They resisted a wild urge to do what others had done, to fall down and kiss the ground under the flagpole. A British police officer (an Indian) examined their passports which were six months expired. Nervously Amy chattered, "We thought you might turn us back!"

With real friendliness, he replied, "*We* wouldn't turn you back. *We* welcome you!" She nearly hugged him. These were the first kind words they'd heard for a long time.

A New Zealand colleague, Edna McLaren, met them at the border with tea and sandwiches. Then, after an hour's train ride, they alighted at the Kowloon Station where a large crowd of mission friends waited with open arms to receive them. They felt enveloped in love, even though they walked around in a daze for quite some time.

The Macs and Mary were the last New Zealanders in the CIM to leave China. The news was broadcast over the NZ national radio network. At Geraldine, the Morrisons and we four older children listened to the news brief with tears running down our faces. In darker moments, we had wondered if we would ever see Mother and Dad again.

In their first letter to prayer partners, Norman and Amy wrote: "Only those who have been through a similar experience can understand the long, dreary days and nights, when Satan has power to tempt, and the icy fingers of fear clutch at the heart and seek to paralyze. It was then that your prayers counted so much, and again and again we were conscious of being helped to victory and deliverance on the wave of someone's prayers. Thank you."

Naturally, Norman and Amy were keen to get on to New Zealand and the waiting children immediately, but this was not to be.

"You've no idea how strange you people are when you come from inland," laughed one of the leaders, no doubt referring to their disoriented behaviour rather than their unfashionable clothes. So, for those who had been waiting a long time to get "out" there was a routine procedure to follow. First, a very necessary period of rest and relaxation was prescribed. The Macs went with others for a month to Cheung Chao Island, an hour's ferry ride down Hong Kong Harbour. This was a wise move as it gave them not only time to recover physically and emotionally, but helped restore a sense of perspective before they had to face audiences in the West.

Norman and Amy never knew who made the provision for them to travel First Class to New Zealand, but they truly praised God for this unexpected treat. Unfortunately, a day out of port, they ran into the tail end of a typhoon and were severely buffeted. Their cabin was awash, and as they lay seasick and uncaring, they could hear their suitcases swishing and crashing back and forth across the floor. Only after three turbulent days did they enter calmer waters, and oh, that lovely moment when they could open the porthole and breathe in the fresh sea air!

In Sydney they attended a church where Principal Morling, of the Baptist College, was to preach. Hearing that they were in the congregation, just arrived from China, he changed his sermon, and spoke on "The Insomnia of God." As they heard the lovely words of Psalm 121 expounded, "He who keeps you will not slumber. Behold, He who keeps Israel will neither slumber nor sleep," the tears of gratitude flowed, for Norman and Amy knew it was true. God had been awake and watchful, caring for them all through the past long years of strain.

Twinkle was very thrilled with everything she saw and the many experiences that came her way for the first time. Norman and Amy hadn't realized just how much she had missed the company of other children through their being incommunicado from national friends. One day, while seated at the window of her aunt's house in Sydney, she saw children running down the street after school, and jumped up in great excitement.

"Children, auntie," she begged, stretching out her hands. "Catch one!"

She was soon to have all the playmates she could manage. The family settled in Gore, a small country town in the far south of New Zealand.

With the birth of Lesley Mary, several months later, the family was complete. Truly God had kept and blessed us all! Amy's favourite hymn at this time was, "Forever here my rest shall be!" With joyful anticipation, she looked forward to the years ahead when she would care for her large brood and enter into our daily joys and sorrows as we grew up. She neither expected nor desired to leave New Zealand again.

CHAPTER 11

A NEW BEGINNING

T he family soon dropped into its furlough routine.
Norman ranged the length and breadth of the land telling
what the Lord had done. After his year with God in prison, he
went out with God in power, and people everywhere
responded to his message. Adults and children were converted, young people received their call to Christian service,
and believers were challenged to take new steps of faith.

It was wonderful to be alive and free, free to preach the
gospel again.

"How did the meeting go tonight?" one of us would ask as
Dad came in the door.

"Rolled 'em in the aisles, dear, rolled 'em in the aisles!"
he would say jokingly.

"Tell us what happened!" we'd beg, eager to hear what
new thing God had done that night. As the stories were told,
it was clear to see how grateful and humbled Dad felt to be
used by God like this.

He would sometimes be away for weeks at a stretch. Such
a far-flung ministry was only possible for him because Mother
was willing to make the sacrifice of staying at home with the
family. Most of the time she cared for us six children
single-handed. It was a heavy responsibility but I don't ever
recall her complaining. She kept home a happy, cheerful
place. But we particularly relished the periods when Dad was
home, and there'd be a general scramble for his attention.

He was a great person to talk to, and very understanding, if you could get him to stop still long enough to listen. I would offer to accompany him to deputation meetings out in the country, not because I was eager to hear the same message for the tenth time, but because he would be pinned behind the steering wheel for an hour either way. All mine for two hours! We had some marvellous talks.

Dad could always see the other fellow's point of view. When the freezer workers went on strike and all our farmer friends were clamouring for their blood, Dad dared to put in a word for the scoundrels.

For years, Mother adamantly refused to buy anything produced by Communist China. But, "I don't think we can take that line," Dad would reason. "Even people in Communist China have to live."

None of us knew how long we would be "on furlough." Obviously, the mission would want to use Dad in deputation for a while longer. After that? We didn't know but fully expected that God would have a job for him to do in New Zealand. Then we would all settle down to "normal family life." We were looking forward to it.

During the year Dad and Mother had been detained in China, a momentous decision had been made by CIM leaders. The China Inland Mission, as such, would cease to exist. It was to be renamed the Overseas Missionary Fellowship (OMF) and its workers redeployed to serve in the countries surrounding China to the east and south. Their first goal would be to reach the millions of Chinese who lived throughout the region, but new work was also to be commenced among other races.

One of these countries was Malaya (now Malaysia), which had been torn for several years by civil war. Just under half the population was Chinese, with slightly more Malays. The remainder was composed of a miscellany of races, though mostly Indian. Communist terrorists were making a determined bid to overthrow the government (then British) and were being supplied with food and other necessities by the local Chinese, many of whom were relatives.

In an attempt to break the supply lines and cripple the terrorists, the government had forcibly removed all the Chinese squatters from the edges of the jungle where, for years, they had planted their garden plots, and had gathered them into new villages. These jerrybuilt clusters of houses were surrounded by high barbed-wire fences, lit with arc lights, guarded by police and controlled by curfews and other restrictions. Officially, all this was to protect the citizens. But, not surprisingly, the action had generated great resentment and ill-will.

While we were enjoying furlough and family life at home in New Zealand, the officer commanding Malaya, Sir Gerald Templer, sent out an urgent call for one hundred missionaries, immediately, to go and live in the new villages to show the people "a better way of life." Communism could not be countered with guns alone. When the news reached us in Gore, we were excited about it. What an opportunity! Daily in our family devotions, we took turns asking God to stir up people to go.

But was prayer the only response God wanted from us? One morning Averil came to where Mother was cooking at the stove.

"Mother," she said without preamble, "I think you ought to go back!"

"What?" cried Amy, with a touch of resentment. "Don't you like having us home and all being together?"

"Of course I do," she answered rather hesitantly, "but ..."

"But what? Why do you think we ought to go back?"

"Well," came the reply, "you and Daddy do have the language, and there are so many people in Malaya who have never heard the gospel." With that she vanished, leaving a very disturbed mother at the stove.

Try as she would, Amy couldn't shake off this unpalatable suggestion. She had an uncomfortable feeling that this was more than the mere personal opinion of a thoughtless thirteen-year-old. Should it be from God, was she willing to listen and obey?

The struggle was fierce. I watched her in church one morning, at Communion, with her eyes closed and tears running down her cheeks. Jesus had died for her. Could she not give herself to Him?

At this point, Dad arrived home from an extensive and successful deputation tour. He was tired but exuberant. Now, to be met by this! He felt as though a bucket of cold water had been thrown over him.

Go back? To a country threatened by Communism? No, a thousand times no! He remembered the Communist interrogations, and afterwards, when his bed had shaken for hours as tangled nerves relaxed. They had been through enough. They couldn't face such a situation again. It shouldn't be expected of them.

In any case, there was a perfectly legitimate reason why they could not go. Surely their first responsibility was to care for the children God had given them. But, even while they argued back and forth, they recognized the Spirit's Voice in their hearts.

"Yes, it was I who spoke to you through your daughter. I want you to go with Me to Malaya. Don't be so troubled and afraid. You can trust Me. You know I will never let you down."

The very next morning came a letter from Geraldine. Jack and Lois Morrison wrote, "We want you to know that, if ever you feel the Lord is asking you to return to Asia, we would be willing to take your five older children — and care for them as our own, until such time as you can take them again."

When they read that, Norman and Amy just gazed at each other dumbly. They were without excuse! They could no longer say "can't." God was holding them to their promise to obey, and had again proved Himself faithful as the Provider.

So the Morrisons became our guardians once more. Although we love them dearly, they never usurped the position of our parents. The relationship is different. But they gave us something else most precious — a stable home base. The word "family" conjures up delightful images of togetherness in many places. The word "home" brings up the picture of a certain red-brick house on the Geraldine Downs. To this day, a warm welcome awaits us whenever we return. The scents, sounds and memories of past years enfold us. We love the place. It is home.

Norman and Amy were sincerely and deeply grateful to the Lord for this wonderful provision, and to the Morrisons who, through their unpossessive love and godly example, were to shepherd us safely through our teenage years. But it was never easy, especially for Amy, to accept this ambiguity of allegiance.

Until this time, even when we children were at Chefoo, there had been no doubt about where home was. Home was where our parents were. But from now on, this would change. The most painful sacrifice of Amy's life as a mother, was to relinquish her "right" to bring up her own children. It was a recurring sacrifice which never got any easier. Once again, however, came the familiar words of reassurance, "He is worthy for whom you should do this."

So, early in 1954, while the shooting war was still raging in Malaya, Norman and Amy, with Lesley who was now a toddler, arrived in Singapore on an Italian passenger liner. After a few days at the Overseas Missionary Fellowship headquarters, they went on by train to Kuala Lumpur, where they learned of their designation to Gemas Bahru.

Immediately they got into Malaya, they felt oppressed by the sultry heat which steamed up from the jungles, oppressed also by the prevailing atmosphere of fear and uncertainty. Gemas Bahru was a small village almost on the border of Johore and Negeri Sembilan States. Norman and Amy were thankful to arrive unharmed at their little rented, rough-hewn shack.

There were no drains, no running water, and for some time, no electricity either. But the concrete floor was convenient and could be cleaned easily by swishing a pail of water over it. Under the unlined tin roof the place was like an oven until it rained, and then they could hardly hear themselves think for the din. To add to its special features, the roof leaked!

Amy cooked on a small, two-burner kerosene stove. A portable camp oven could be fitted over one burner for baking. "So now," she quipped, "we shall be able to roast the hind leg of a cobra for a treat!"

The wall-boards were divided by cracks and didn't quite reach the floor. So, while lizards ran up and down the walls, toads often slipped into the rooms at ground level, occasionally followed by a hungry snake. Other unwelcome livestock were centipedes, scorpions and cockroaches.

Water was carried from the village well and stored in large crocks — one in the kitchen and one in the tiny bath house alongside. Like everyone else in the village, Norman and Amy had several baths a day just to keep cool. Frequent washing also discouraged prickly heat and skin funguses. The bathing procedure was a new experience. The bather stood on a concrete slab and, after lathering, sloshed dippers full of cold water over himself to rinse off.

Fortunately the Macs didn't have to wait too long before electricity was connected to the house and they were able to power some fans. When Norman turned on the radio for the first time, a voice announced, "Wait on the Lord. Be of good courage, and He shall strengthen thine heart." What a surprise! They had happened on a programme being broadcast from the Far East Broadcasting Company in Manila.

These heartening words were the Lord's message to them as they started work in Gemas Bahru. Not only were the living conditions tough, but apart from the village chairman who had welcomed them cordially enough, the people were generally unfriendly and suspicious. What were these westerners doing in the village? Were they agents of the government, even spies perhaps? "Keep your distance, everyone. Tell these foreigners nothing. Avoid contact with them."

Norman and Amy felt this isolation keenly and prayed daily that the Lord would break down the barrier of hostility. They were pleased when they received an invitation to the village school concert. Some five hundred people were jammed into the school hall when the headmaster ushered the foreigners on to a front bench.

Impromptu, he called on Amy to sing. Her mind went a complete blank! Norman, without a blush, stepped into the breach and gave a spirited, if not accurate, rendering of "Where have you been, Billy Boy?" The crowd roared its approval, though no one there would have understood a word of it. After this, there was a definite improvement in the overall attitude of the villagers towards their western neighbours.

The Macs prayed for friends and took every possible opportunity to show the people that they loved them. They offered medical help. One day, in a fight, a boy broke a bowl of rice over the head of his young brother. The lad arrived bleeding heavily from a deep cut behind his ear and with rice still sticking to his hair!

Another time a girl's foot needed three stitches. Then there was the sad occasion when a woman went into difficult labour giving birth to twins. "Come quickly," panted a messenger to Norman. But they had waited too long to call him. When he got there, she was dead and her six children were left motherless.

At a town some miles to the south there was a hospital. The Macs had a small van and willingly made their services available in case of emergency to take patients there. If the call came at night, the journey could be a hair-raising experience. All roads were under curfew during the hours of dark, so Norman was often checked at road blocks. As terrorists frequently crossed the highway under cover of darkness and sometimes put up their own road blocks, he could never be quite sure who was stopping him, the police or the enemy!

Bit by bit, people began to trust them. An old vegetable seller wept as he told how his son had been whisked off to prison. There were deep sorrows in many lives, families torn apart by the war, brothers fighting against brothers. The people were bound by fear, fear of the terrorists on the human level and fear of the spirits on the supernatural level.

Their lives were so terrifyingly dark and loveless. Norman and Amy tried to tell them about the Saviour who could heal their wounds and bring them light and gladness, but they couldn't hear, they wouldn't listen. They seemed unable to understand. How the Macs prayed against this spirit of unbelief.

After the wide open spaces of Tibet, it was a cramping experience to be living in a guarded village, under curfew from six in the evening until six the next morning, at which hour the rubber tappers went off to the estates to work. They were permitted to carry only a bottle of clear tea, and all suffered a body search as they passed through the village gates. It was prohibited to take any food with them as this might come into the hands of the guerillas.

In spite of such stringent preventive measures, however, the people found many ingenious ways to circumvent this veto. After all, blood is thicker than water and some of them had relatives out in the jungles desperate for food. There were shops in Gemas township where it was possible to purchase tinned foods. But every tin had to be punctured before it left the shop, or carried back to the village with a police permit.

The eight hundred inhabitants of Gemas Bahru spoke, between them, seven or more dialects and languages. Although there was a sprinkling of Indians, most were Chinese. Norman and Amy had to manage as best they could in Mandarin, which they had learned in China. Fortunately, the schools used Mandarin, so even if communication with some of the older dialect-speakers was difficult, the missionaries could always speak directly to the younger folk.

For a while they groped around for some kind of work pattern or routine. They felt the need to get their teeth into something tangible and definite. But their ministry in the village refused to take shape and continued to be a frustrating mess of bits and pieces.

Partly as a result of this, the Macs found themselves

looking over the barbed wire into the surrounding rubber estates where thousands of Tamil-speaking Indians lived and worked as tappers. Possibly because Tamil was a Sanskrit language, and not unlike Tibetan in its written form, they felt especially drawn to it and to the poor, neglected people who spoke it.

"By faith" they started learning Tamil, but the action was premature. The directors of the mission had, at that stage, made no decision to start Tamil work, and so the Macs were asked to switch to Cantonese, one of the most common of the Chinese dialects.

Life in the village was a kaleidoscope which changed minute by minute. making an ordered programme impossible. From this perspective, they saw the ministry of Jesus in a new way.

"Have you ever noticed," asked Amy one day, "how so much of the Lord's dealing with people was 'unplanned'? Some of His greatest works were done in response to interruptions."

As they looked up Scriptures together, they discovered that a number of significant encounters occurred "as He was going in the way," or "as He passed by." Not when He got there, but almost casually was the real work done.

This encouraged them to look at their piecemeal ministry with new eyes. They asked their supporters to pray that they would be kept awake, not to miss the cue when it came, and to regard interruptions as potential opportunities.

They did what they could in aggressive evangelistic outreach. Amy ran a Sunday School class to which some fifty boisterous youngsters came off and on. After each session she'd be hoarse.

In the comparative cool of the evening, people would wander about the narrow streets, eating and chatting. There wasn't much to do in the village by way of recreation. Every Wednesday evening, Norman would hook up the pressure lamp outside their front door, hang up a poster on the wall and begin to preach.

He used local illustrations as much as possible. Now and again, government planes would roar overhead sowing the jungle with Safe Conduct Passes. Simultaneously, a loud voice from the sky would blare out the offer of amnesty to any terrorist soldier who would come out of the jungle, carrying his gun high and holding a pass. He would be guaranteed safety and a full pardon. Norman got hold of one of these passes.

"You all know what this is," he said one Wednesday evening, waving the leaflet in the air. "Tonight I want to tell you about the safe conduct pass God has provided for us to go to heaven."

Inevitably a crowd would gather around to listen, though from a distance. Most people hid in the shadows for fear of being identified by Communist informers. There was often active opposition. Boys would attach a strip of rubber to the back wheel of their bicycles and spin the wheel to make a screeching sound that all but drowned out the preacher. Others sneaked around behind the listeners, burning the backs of their legs with lighted cigarettes.

Wednesday after Wednesday, Norman and Amy would drop into their bed worn out and discouraged. How could they keep on like this?

Norman ordered a public address system to amplify the message. The Macs nicknamed it "Aaron" because it became the mouthpiece of Moses and also helped "Hur!" But one night, Norman gave a very solemn message on The Flood. With all his heart, he warned the people, "The Spirit of God will not always strive with man. He will not always strive with you!" His words were resented, and someone maliciously knocked Aaron over and smashed the microphone.

The going had been so hard, but with this incident, suddenly the ambassadors of Christ felt very down. Would anyone ever believe in the Lord? The answer, in their *Daily Light* reading, came as a drink of water to a thirsty soul. "It is good that a man both *hope* and *wait quietly* for the salvation of the Lord" (Lamentations 3:25,26). They asked their prayer partners to help them do both.

While the villagers went their hardhearted way, apparently unmoved, Norman and Amy were encouraged by some positive response from people outside Gemas Bahru. Norman obtained permission to hold weekly meetings in the one Chinese and three Tamil schools on a nearby Dunlop estate. This estate covered nine thousand acres and was served by 72 miles of laterite roads which could become treacherous when it rained. That was not the only hazard. Often as he travelled alone through the rubber trees, Norman felt his skin prickle with apprehension, but God protected him from any sniper attack, and the school children listened eagerly to his teaching.

Outside the village they met British personnel in various capacities, and took every opportunity to tell them also about Christ. They were overjoyed when a Red Cross nurse put her faith in Jesus as Saviour.

The difficulties Norman and Amy encountered at Gemas Bahru were not unique. Their feelings of frustration and personal inadequacy were shared by fellow workers in other new villages. One of their greatest encouragements at this time was to visit other colleagues or be visited in turn, for days of prayer together or for reciprocal ministry. Just to know they were not alone in this warfare was, in itself, a strength.

They returned from one such visit to find their almost-ready-to-eat tomatoes all stolen, and three pots of maidenhair fern stripped. These had been so pretty and had helped to beautify their ugly dwelling. The thief had broken into the house but evidently, finding no money, had departed, venting his annoyance by this bit of vandalism.

About the same time, who should pop in for morning tea but Mr J O Sanders and his wife! As the new General Director of OMF, he was making a trip around the new fields, and brought his usual cheer. They thought of the many and varied experiences they had shared with him, and were reminded again of the pilgrim nature of their lives as they read together the small plaque that hung on the wall of the living area, "This too shall pass away."

It was important to keep things in an eternal perspective, but in the meantime, this raucous, resistant little village was the context in which they had to live and work. Their ministry went on, always overshadowed by the activities of the terrorists. One morning, the villagers awoke to find the body of a British officer strung up on the barbed-wire fence "as an example." Another day, a young woman rubber tapper was carried in. Terrorists had surprised her at work and tortured her by shredding her calf muscles to ribbons.

The guerillas killed the language teacher of missionaries in a nearby village, and also the daughter of the one professing Christian family who had previously lived in Gemas Bahru. Clearly it was dangerous to have anything to do with the foreigners or with Christianity. The chairman of the village, earlier quite friendly, was now scarcely civil. The Macs suspected he'd been warned off, or else! Many of the people who had listened to the preaching at first, now stopped coming. The opposition of the adversary was relentless.

He attacked the Mac's language teacher another way. One day when Norman was out, the man rushed to the house calling for him, then rushed away again without saying what was the trouble. They found out the awful truth later. His wife had drunk caustic soda and died in agony. Why? She had taken to playing mahjongg and arriving home around eleven at night, and her husband had reprimanded her. She left four small children.

Norman had been doing quite a bit of photographic work for OMF home centres for use in publications and missionary deputation. For this he had two cameras, both quite valuable. One day, he discovered they had disappeared from the cubicle he used as an office. His heart sank. Frantically, he searched through the rest of the house, just in case. But no, they'd gone. Someone had stolen them.

The Macs felt sick about this. To lose the cameras was bad enough, but to have them go over the fence into the wrong hands was worse still. Norman reported the theft to the authorities and then he and Amy got down on their knees before the unseen Authority.

"O God," they requested, "we're looking to You for a miracle. We want the cameras returned!"

Somehow the news of their loss leaked out and before long the whole village knew about it. With a heavy heart, Norman hung up his pressure lamp that Wednesday night and started to preach. There was an unusually large attendance. Was the thief there among the crowd?

At dawn a day or two later, Norman and Amy were woken by the shrill cries of children.

"Your cameras are here! Your cameras are here!"

They rushed into the backyard in their night clothes. Sure enough, there were the cameras. They'd been thrown over the fence. Norman picked them up and was amazed to find that they were quite undamaged.

Joy welled up in their hearts. God had heard and answered their prayer. He had intervened in an impossible situation.

This incident so encouraged them that Norman took some time to write to Alastair telling the story in detail. He also mentioned how, for many months, they had been treating a young rubber tapper for a tropical ulcer on her shin. Not only was the ulcer slow to heal, but the girl's heart didn't seem to get any softer towards the gospel.

Some weeks later, the Macs were surprised to receive an anonymous letter from Sydney, Australia, addressed to "The Parents of Alastair."

"I have just returned from a holiday in New Zealand," they read. "While there we went to Mt Cook by tourist bus and stopped at Geraldine for refreshments. I found your letter to Alastair lying on the footpath. Not knowing where to send it, I took it with me. It made fascinating reading! Please accept the enclosed gift for the patient with the tropical ulcer." The Macs often wondered about the man who wrote that letter, but there was never any further word from him.

That year the monsoon was unusually heavy. Just before Christmas, torrential rain fell causing widespread flooding. It was eerie to see practically submerged trees with snakes and lizards waving from their topmost branches. Norman helped evacuate villagers from the lower-lying areas and house them temporarily in the school. The village was completely cut off and people were growing very apprehensive as the waters continued to rise.

Staying with the Macs at the time was Superintendent Percy Moore, on one of his periodic visits, and he was forced to stay on until the waters subsided. At the very first opportunity, he made for Gemas town to fill up his petrol tank, so that he could hurry back to important engagements in Kuala Lumpur. The car wouldn't go. He discovered that his tank had been filled, not with petrol, but with water. The underground fuel tanks had also been inundated!

The Macs were invited to Kuala Lumpur for Christmas, but decided, in view of the floods, to stay with the people in the village and lend a hand with the cleanup. During a pause in the rain, a parcel was delivered. It was a gramophone record from the Morrisons at Geraldine with a word each from Alastair, Gavin and Twinkle. Both boys played the piano, Gav and Twink sang — all beautifully clear. It was such an unexpected surprise.

With tears and laughter they played this masterpiece over and over. Somehow the "empty" Christmas they'd anticipated wasn't so empty any more. The little house was, after all, filled with the voices of their children.

That year a Christian bookstore was opened in Kuala Lumpur, the first in the whole of Malaya. It was the Evangel Book Centre. The only significance this had for Norman at the time was that it would make it much easier to get supplies of Christian literature for their work. At Chinese New Year, he obtained a calendar and tract for delivery to every home in the village.

By then, the Macs had been in Gemas Bahru for almost a year, and still they knew of no one who had believed in Jesus through their efforts. Time and again they encouraged each other with the Lord's promise, "My word shall not return to me void." There must be people in Gemas Bahru who belonged to Christ. One day they would find their Saviour. Perhaps even now there were some secret believers. What a cheer it would be to know of even one.

Lesley used to play for hours of the day in a small tub of water. With her fluffy, blond hair and blue eyes, she was a continual attraction to the local children who had uniformly straight, black hair and brown eyes. One of these became a special friend. Little A-Kai, whose parents had been deported to China, lived with her granny in the Old People's Home opposite. She came regularly to Amy's Sunday School and played with Lesley whenever she could.

Thirteen years later, on a visit to Kuala Lumpur, the Macs attended the city-wide evangelistic crusade organized by the Billy Graham Association. One memorable night, after a meeting, a young woman came up to them and said,

"Do you remember me? I'm A-Kai from Gemas Bahru."

"A-Kai! What are you doing here?"

"I first heard about Jesus from you," she replied, "and asked Him to be my Saviour. Now I am a student at Bible School preparing to be a Christian worker myself."

The staff at the Bible School declared she was one of their best open-air preachers. Could those bedlam preaching sessions in Gemas Bahru have given some inspiration after all? Now here she was, a singer in the large Crusade Choir and a trained counsellor, competent to lead others to the Saviour.

With grateful hearts Norman and Amy remembered the Scripture which says, "Cast your bread upon the waters, for after many days you will find it again" (Ecclesiastes 11:1). That gruelling year in Gemas Bahru had borne fruit after all!

CHAPTER 12

GOD'S SALESMAN

"**N**orman," came the request from headquarters, "would you be willing to leave Gemas Bahru now? We want you to come to Singapore to head up a distribution programme for Christian Witness Press." This was the OMF literature arm.

Literature? he thought. *Leave real missionary work to market literature? Surely direct evangelism is more worthy a calling. So much of my missionary life already has been taken up in these service ministries. Can this be right?*

He and Amy were uncertain. "Lord," they prayed, "we accept this directive as from You, but we ask for Your personal reassurance."

For some time Norman had been suffering bouts of back pain which he jokingly referred to as his "plumbago." Now the pain became so intense he had to go to Singapore for tests. These showed a displaced disc, so after a stint in Singapore General Hospital, he was discharged in a full trunk plaster. The next nine weeks were a super-tropical experience!

He itched incessantly and yearned for the day when he could take a bath. Meanwhile Amy and Lesley did their best to relieve his misery by scratching him with a knitting needle, the only instrument thin enough to get between the plaster and the victim.

At the same time, the position of hostess at the Singapore mission home became vacant. Unexpectedly, Amy was asked to take over the job.

Clearly, the Lord had answered their prayer for guidance. The decision to move from Gemas Bahru had been taken right out of their hands. While Norman recuperated, Amy set about housekeeping. In addition to a regular contingent of 23 headquarters staff, she had to provide hospitality for a constant stream of visitors. The relentless heat and crowded conditions often caused nerves to fray.

One day, Amy was in the pantry putting away some groceries. She sensed someone behind her and turned around. The Director of Finance was standing in the doorway. Funds were low and economy was being urged. She imagined he was looking at her accusingly and thought guiltily of the few "luxury" items she'd just stowed away along with the bargains and dented cans. *Oh, get off my back,* she muttered inwardly. *How can I do this job if you're always breathing down my neck?*

On another occasion, there was pineapple for lunch. Amy decided to slice it in rings thinking it would look prettier that way. As dessert came on to the table, a querulous voice was raised. "Who was the stupid person who cut the pineapple like this? It's not fair because some people get sweet slices and others get sour. Anyone knows you should cut pineapple lengthwise!"

The hostess crept away and cried. Why couldn't people be nice? Why couldn't they even act grown-up? She was doing her best to make things attractive and pleasant for them, and all she got was ingratitude and criticism!

Often she felt swamped and inadequate in such tight community living and was acutely aware of the graces she lacked. This threw her into a greater reliance on the Lord and, in His strength, she found she was able to overcome self-pity and cope with the daily stresses without being negative towards others.

This was to be an interim job for her, however. About the time Norman came out of plaster, she fell ill with diptheria. The acute stage of the illness passed, but leaving her with weak heart muscles, and a long time of convalescence was anticipated before she could hope to get back on her feet again. Mrs Sanders took over the housekeeping while the patient was moved to the home of friends in another part of the city.

Thank God for this comfortable bed anyway, Amy thought gratefully as she lay there in utter weakness day after day. A rubber mattress was something of a luxury in those days when most people slept on hard, and often lumpy, kapok. Almost a year before Norman's back played up and she became ill, a friend had felt God prompting him to send the Macs a Dunlopillo mattress. The gift was a cheering reminder of their Master's loving care and foreknowledge.

Its provision was a small thing, perhaps, but it helped to anchor them in this time of testing when, like Job, they were tempted to cry, "All these things are against me!" At the same time, they were convinced that these crippling attacks on their health came from the Evil One, to keep them from the Lord's work. They held fast to the belief that in these trials God was working His sovereign purposes out, although they couldn't see how.

As Amy lay recuperating, she longed for something worthwhile and creative to do. An earlier request to write a book on Malaya had been put aside for lack of time. Now, in weakness, she wrote *Journey into Malaya*. It was a largely autobiographical novel which described the spiritual struggle that was going on in the new villages of Malaya. Not only did this book stimulate prayer for the village work, but Amy was cheered to learn later of some readers who had found Christ through it.

Norman, chafing at his enforced inactivity, prowled round the literature store room checking supplies. Obviously, he was going to have to find better ways to preserve stock from bugs and humidity. "Cockroaches seem to show a greater hunger for the printed page than the average Christian," he reported to Amy.

It soon became clear to him that his major task would be to find effective ways to distribute this material. Much of it consisted of evangelistic tracts and posters in Chinese, so he began with these. As soon as he was cut out of his plaster and his back was strong enough, he started to visit Chinese churches to challenge pastors to use this literature more widely in their evangelistic efforts.

They weren't interested and made excuses. "The posters are too expensive," they objected. But Norman pressed on, refusing to be defeated. At last, one young pastor became infected with Norman's enthusiasm. He launched out and purchased two hundred posters and three thousand tracts. The whole church was mobilized. Members displayed posters in their windows, shop fronts and doorways. They gave out tracts and witnessed to Jesus, and the response was tremendous. Now other churches were shown a successful model and they followed suit. The project took off in a big way.

Norman, mightily encouraged, set off on a combined preaching and selling trip into Malaya. He preached the Word and sold the Scriptures. He demonstrated how to use the posters and how to give out tracts. Here and there he met people who had been converted through reading a Christian book. As a result of his efforts, he saw others go out witnessing with renewed purpose and zeal, their hands full of tracts. With growing excitement, it dawned on him that the Lord was launching him into a most powerful form of ministry.

Joyfully he discovered that he was tailor-made for the job. He loved this kind of work. Far from being only a backup service for others, a literature ministry could be just as direct and as personal as he cared to make it.

"Norman, you missed your calling!" exclaimed Jack Clingleffer, chairman of the Evangel Book Centre, some time later. "You should have been a salesman, not a missionary!"

On his first furlough, Norman had turned his back on a tempting offer to become a secular salesman and had doggedly renewed his missionary commitment in obedience to Christ. Back in China, the Lord had trained him in business management and book keeping. He had sweated it out as an evangelist at the grass-roots level in China, Tibet and Malaya. And how frustrated he had often felt because of the patchwork nature of his experience. He seemed to be a Jack-of-all-trades but master of none.

Suddenly now, all the strands of his life seemed to be coming together. Here was a ministry he could get his teeth into, one that demanded all he had in ability and experience. Certainly a few cupboards of stock was not a large beginning, but faith refused to be limited by present realities. In Norman's heart there grew a vision of what might be.

He remembered how he himself, as an ignorant teenager only two days old in the Christian faith, had been so profoundly influenced by the biography, *George Muller of Bristol*. A few years later, God had confirmed His call to China through another book, *Rusty Hinges*. This was the power of the printed page!

What were new believers reading in Malaya? Communist books? It was illegal of course, but the brightly-coloured tracts and posters proclaiming salvation through hate and revolution were available everywhere. The message of God's love through the Cross was largely unknown.

"O God," Norman cried, "what can we do to remedy this situation?"

The vision of literature for Malaya was not Norman's alone, but was the deep concern of the Fellowship. The Evangel Book Centre (EBC), in Kuala Lumpur, was the only Christian bookstore in Malaya. It came into being largely through the vision of Kenneth Price, another OMF missionary who, incidentally, had been the mastermind behind the Christian Witness Press as well. EBC was financed by a group of local businessmen but managed by the Prices.

After only nine months in Singapore, Norman was asked to take charge of the Evangel Book Centre while the Prices went on furlough. To be a roving salesman, working on his own, was one thing. To be manager of an operation involving others was another. With considerable diffidence, he moved north to the new appointment. The shift was complicated by the fact that Amy was still very weak and Norman had to take full responsibility for looking after three-year-old Lesley.

The Macs prayed, "Lord, set Your seal on this move." Almost immediately after they started, a lad came into the store. "I want to know the truth," he told them, and Norman had the joy of leading him to the Saviour.

He was the forerunner of many others, mostly young Buddhists, who came into the store on one pretext or another, but in whose hearts gnawed the same deep longing to know "the truth." These city people were far more open than the village folk had been. The villagers were often barely literate, their minds closed, superstitious and resistant to change. By contrast, these more educated urban people had questioning minds. They were dissatisfied with the old ways, ready to change if they could be convinced that the new way was true and would satisfy.

Norman urged new believers first to buy a Bible and start reading it every day. Then he introduced them to biographies and other books on the Christian life. Because the needs of each inquirer were different, Norman and his colleagues prayed daily that the Lord would make them sensitive and discerning as they served people.

"We are not here just to sell books," he warned his staff. "We must offer the *right* books to each customer. Ours is a spiritual ministry, not a money-making business."

At the same time, he had to wage constant war against the universal concept (hangover from a paternalistic missionary era) that Christian literature should be free or offered at big discounts, and that it was unspiritual for a Christian business to make a profit.

"If we don't sell our books at a reasonable price," he would answer the critics, "we shall not be able to cover running expenses. The store will close and there will be nowhere for you to get your Bibles and books."

Then again, "If we don't make a profit, we shall not be able to expand our stock and our service to you will always be limited."

Unlike in the new villages, there were established churches in the city. In 1956, these churches were largely ignorant of the many aids that were available to strengthen their life and outreach. Norman started an aggressive campaign to introduce them to Christian literature. It meant going out to them in the evenings or at weekends.

This was uphill work at first. The colporteur who desired to display and sell books in the church was opposed, on the grounds that he was just trying to make money out of the members! Here Norman discovered that if he could just get the chance to preach as well as to sell, the book ministry could be demonstrated to his hearers in its spiritual dimension. If they could only see the true worth of Christian books, they would quickly be inspired to read and use them for their own enrichment and witness. Then they would cease to feel they were being exploited.

"Buy two books," he would urge folk enthusiastically, "a book to own and a book to loan! Lending books can be a life-changing ministry."

When he suggested that, even better than having a visiting colporteur would be for a church to operate its own bookstall, he ran into further opposition. "Now," they accused him, "you want us to do your work for you!"

Little by little, he was able to overcome these mis-apprehensions and convince them that such bookstalls would be to their own advantage. He would then warn prospective bookstall operators of likely pitfalls.

"Never feel guilty about *selling* Christian literature, even evangelistic literature. People value what they buy.

"I know people here are expert bargainers. They really know how to apply the pressure, but don't start cutting prices. If you do, you will soon run out of capital and your ministry to your congregation will be finished."

He urged people to read the books they sold. "A persuasive salesman can *sell* a book, but he can't ensure it will be *read*," he would say. "If you can tell a potential buyer how much you enjoyed a particular book yourself and how it helped you, your customer will not only purchase it, but will determine to read it also."

Norman practised what he preached. He had always gained great inspiration from books and loved to read, but his active days left little time for this occupation. As he grew older, he was troubled by persistent insomnia. At first he used to worry about this condition and would, consequently, get up in the morning jaded and weary. Gradually, he realized that he could relax better if he read for a while. The outcome of this was that he read an astonishing number and range of the books he peddled and got to know his stock inside and out.

Years later a prominent Singapore businessman exclaimed, "Norman McIntosh? I remember him. That man was incredible. He knew every book in the shop!"

For the first few months, Norman's efforts were confined to the capital city. All the time, however, the continuing burden of his heart was to get literature out far and wide throughout the land. In the larger provincial towns also there were churches, and thousands of young people in the schools, a ready market for books. In the villages, struggling Christian workers needed to know what visual aids and simple reading materials were available to help them.

Our present staff is stretched to the limit, Norman reasoned, *and I can't be away from the store all the time. We need an able man who can communicate readily with people in dialect and who has a sense of mission. We also need a van.* These needs were brought to God in prayer.

Not long after, a middle-aged man offered his services to EBC. Norman liked him at once and eagerly inquired about his background.

As a boy in China, Kenneth Chow had been gored by a water-buffalo. He was seriously injured and his desperate mother ran with him to some foreign missionaries who happened to be on vacation in the area.

"Please save my son," she pleaded. They gladly took him

in and nursed him through a long illness. When he was finally well again, his mother begged them to keep him. She was very poor. Her boy would have more opportunity with them. And so Kenneth grew up in their home and became a solid Christian.

Now, in Malaya, he was married with a family. He not only spoke English and several Chinese dialects, but was also fluent in the Malay language. Without a doubt he was God's good gift to the work and would make a splendid colporteur.

Norman was urgent to get going, but there was still no transport. One day, in his travels around the city, he saw a small van in someone's yard. It had no wheels and needed painting but he felt it would meet the need. The owner would sell, but Evangel hadn't the money.

Back in New Zealand, I had commenced work as a trainee teacher and had just received my very first pay cheque. *The first-fruits of my earnings,* I thought. *I would like to give this money to God as a thank offering.* Where should I send it? Somehow I felt the Lord prompting me to forward it to EBC. "Please use it for some special project," I wrote to my parents.

Norman almost broke the speed limit racing around to the back street where he had seen "the van." In a few moments it became the property of Evangel Book Centre.

On 27 February 1956, the EBC van, complete with wheels, fresh paint and a sign announcing its purpose, set off for the first of many promotional trips into the surrounding countryside. Sometimes Norman and Kenneth went together, other times they went separately to various states. Whenever possible Norman combined preaching and selling and his ministry was as enthusiastically received as it was delivered. The weekends were the busiest times, often involving several hours' drive between one service and the next.

"My faith was too small," he told folks. "Instead of a van, I ought to have asked God for a helicopter!"

All this time the war continued. There were unpleasant incidents daily. At dawn one day, the Macs nearly jumped out of their skins when, without warning, the Royal Air Force gave a nearby area a very heavy bombing. Clouds of rubble rose up into the sky. The day before, thirteen terrorists had been killed in a similar raid on the Johore jungle. It was a very nasty little war, and not so little either.

On one occasion, Norman had to go to Singapore on the night train. Guerillas were making frequent attacks on the line and it was dangerous. The engine was preceded by an armoured railcar about ten minutes ahead, to save the train should there be explosives or a break in the line. An engineer had once shown Norman the inside of one of these vehicles. In large letters over the front window, for the benefit of the driver, were the words, "Have you received permission to proceed?"

"A good reminder for an activist like me," Norman thought ruefully. "Lord," he prayed, "I know I have a tendency to rush into things and push others into premature action too. Please help me, in each situation, to wait patiently until you give the all-clear."

In various ways the devil tried to dislocate their lives and sabotage the work. He played on their fears. After their China experience they were very vulnerable. Road blocks, curfews and the ever-present danger that lurked in the jungles and rubber plantations through which Norman and Kenneth had to drive, added greatly to the nervous strain of these out-of-town trips. In weak moments, they were often tempted to quit and to stay put in the comparative safety of the city.

The outstation trips could only continue if the supply base kept functioning smoothly. Norman returned from one trip to find the accounts in confusion. The recently-appointed book keeper had turned out to be inept.

Another time, Lesley tumbled into a ten-foot-deep monsoon drain outside the front gate. If a Chinese friend some distance away hadn't seen her disappear, and acted quickly to save her, she would certainly have been drowned.

Then Norman suffered a cruel gall bladder attack, the first in sixteen years. A while later he became ill with a form of amoebic dysentery which left him with a large abcess on the liver.

These trials cast Norman and Amy on the Lord. They were involved in spiritual warfare and they recognized the enemy. Only through prayer could his evil designs be nullified.

In spite of these obstacles, the Lord caused the work to grow rapidly. Before 1956 ended and the Macs went on furlough, a sub-depot was flourishing in Penang. Then came news that a young businessman was planning to run a Christian Book Corner in his office in North Borneo. Many churches were by then operating bookstalls. Gradually, Norman's vision to see Christian literature readily available throughout the land was becoming a reality.

He was not, however, to be involved in the further development of literature outreach in Malaya. After furlough, it was decided, the Macs were to go back to Singapore. Norman was grateful for the valuable experience he had gained during the time with EBC and very eager to start establishing a similar operation in the much larger city in the south.

As he reviewed the 21 years of his missionary service, he thought with joy, *This has been the most satisfying year of my life!* He was glad to be going back to New Zealand at this time to be able to share his vision with prayer partners.

When the Macs arrived once more at Gore for furlough, they found a delicious hot meal ready in the oven, the table set and a large iced cake, decorated with the words "Welcome Home." The church friends had once again found a suitable house and paid rent on it for three months to keep it for them. But there was a snag. For only the second time in their association with the mission, general funds were so low that there was no personal allowance for that quarter.

When, as would-be missionaries, Norman and Amy had applied to the China Inland Mission, they were presented with a copy of the Principles and Practice of the CIM. Speaking of financial matters, this manual stated "The Mission may fail, God never." So, while they would be grateful for any remittance from the mission, made possible by the freewill offerings of the Lord's people, they must never count on it. And when it was not what was regarded as a "full remittance," they should seek the Lord in the matter. He, not the mission, was their Provider. So now, with no remittance, they just looked to see what God would do.

Here they were, a father and mother with a large family. Four of us were teenagers with appetites like bottomless pits and growing expenses. Could God once again supply?

While we were eating the welcome-home meal, there came a knock at the door. One of the officers of our local church stood there, smiling. He said, "I work in the freezing works and can buy meat at discount. Could you use any extra meat?" Could we?! This man, for the duration of furlough, provided most of our meat, normally one of the most expensive items on the budget.

He had scarcely departed, when the door knocker sounded again. It was another officer from the church. "I have a baker's shop in town. Just come down and get all the bread you need — anytime!" All the bread we needed! The Lord had promised to supply our daily bread, but in this case, we were invited to help ourselves to the unsold cakes and other baked goodies every weekend as well!

We were also given butter from many farms, and bags of swedes, potatoes and other winter vegetables. These kept us going until our own vegetable garden started producing some months later.

What had been Mother's home church in the North Island for many years, sent a magnificent consignment of tinned goods. "This was so unexpected," she wrote to her mother, "it took our breaths away. So it seems the Lord would say, 'Get on with My work and don't make housekeeping an excuse for refusing to speak!'"

Mother therefore closed her eyes to the muddle in our very crowded house, entertained scores of visitors and spoke at countless meetings around the Southland area. Her greatest pleasure was two weekly classes for Religious Instruction, conducted in a local primary school, and the Girls' Crusader group she led each week in the Gore High School for some eighty to one hundred girls. As usual, Dad was in great demand as a speaker. From Sunday School classes to Keswick Convention, he was on the go all the time and enjoyed a fruitful ministry.

Towards the end of the year came an unexpected letter from headquarters. "Plans have changed. We may not proceed with an expanded literature programme in Singapore at this time. Would you be willing to relieve John Robinson for a year at OMF Publishers, Philippines? Please respond immediately."

The answer had to be "Yes", of course, but it was a keen disappointment. "Oh, Lord, what is this all about?" queried His servants. "We were so sure You wanted us to go to Singapore. What has gone wrong? And here we are being asked to do another temporary job, take another stopgap appointment. This time we were so looking forward to building something ourselves on a more longterm basis."

The Macs had made many friends in Malaya and Singapore and had established good contacts for ministry. Now they were to go to a completely new environment to start all over again. At 46 years of age, they were conscious of being a little less flexible, a little less willing for major changes.

Norman had his own anxieties. OMF Publishers, established three years earlier, was a much larger and more complex operation than EBC. How could he take over its management? Other staff members would know more about it than he did! The old fear of possible failure reared its head once more.

But the Lord stilled their agitated hearts. "Trust Me," he said. "The responsibility is Mine. Your job is to respond to My ability. I will never let you down."

An almost-forgotten fragment of conversation resurfaced in Norman's mind. "We recognize and value the variety of gifts in our workers. Some are thinkers, others are doers.

Both will contribute in their own way."

Men like Ken Price and John Robinson are the thinkers and planners, he thought humbly. *I am a doer. It is my job to build on the foundations they have so ably laid. Every man to his gift. We are a team. Thank you, Lord, for this reminder.*

Before the decision was finally taken, Dad and Mother called a family council and invited us all to put our cards on the table. They would not go back without the willing consent of each one of us. We were all to be in the missionary endeavour together. To consult us children in this way was caring and wise. It reassured us that we were important to our parents. It also made us active participants in the Lord's calling.

After their departure, a woman who ought to have known better than to encourage resentment towards our parents, tried to comfort me. "You poor little things!" she said. "It's terrible the way your parents have gone off and left you like this!"

"Oh no," I was able to assure her, "they didn't leave us, we sent them!"

Such decisions, however, are costly and painful. If we hadn't had the Master's particular promise, how could any of us have done it? "Truly, I say to you, there is no one who has left ... mother or father or children ... for my sake and the gospel who will not receive a hundredfold now in this time ... and in the age to come eternal life" (Mark 9:29-30).

CHAPTER 13 "MR LITERATURE!"

Philippines, "Pearl of the Orient!" What enticing pictures the title conjures up ... bright green paddy fields with cheerful peasants in conical hats chanting at their work, soaring volcanoes, palm-fringed tropical beaches and gentle sea breezes, red sails in the sunset, youths twanging guitars and pretty girls dancing ...

With these in mind, Manila comes as something of a shock to the unprepared. It is steamy, hot and breathless. Squalid, unpainted buildings huddle along endless streets crammed with screeching, honking vehicles. The air is thick with fumes and, everywhere, crowds of people mill aimlessly about. Beautiful old Roman Catholic churches and sleek, luxurious hotels preside over some of the ugliest slums in the world. Norman and Amy were no strangers to human misery, but they were appalled at Tondo where thousands of hapless people actually live on and from the city's refuse dump.

Amy described their home. "Our front fence is about five feet high, and is only a few feet from the front door. Into the cement on top of the fence are embedded many pieces of jagged glass, and at the back of the house several rows of barbed wire. It is also noisy here. We are a few yards from a crossroads, so cars all slow down, tooting and changing gears, and there is a lot of traffic. A large school on one corner has its music room towards us. Street vendors all add to the racket, but first prize goes to the garbage collectors who come every night between twelve and one o'clock. They are a cheerful gang, banging and making merry! They say you get used to noise, and I believe it *could* be possible, but it's going to take time."

It was difficult to adjust to a city like Manila and many times, the Macs found themselves desperately homesick for the mountains of Tibet, the wide open spaces and cool, pure air. Even Kuala Lumpur had been better. There it was green and pleasant, shaded by trees.

"Do we have to work in Manila, Lord?" their hearts cried.

> I said, "Let me walk in the fields."
> He said, "Nay, walk in the town."
> I said, "There are no flowers there."
> He said, "No flowers, but a crown."
> I said, "But the sky is black,
> There is nothing but noise and din."
> But He wept as He sent me back.
> "There is more," He said, "there is sin."
>
> (George MacDonald)

Gradually they got to know and love the Filipinos — such charming, outgoing, warm-hearted people — and they started to put down their roots into this foreign soil.

While English was widely spoken, due to American efforts there since the turn of the century, Tagalog was being promoted as the national language. Norman and Amy decided to become conversant with a few Tagalog sentences which might help them get around more easily. They obtained a copy of the small phrase book which was issued to US servicemen stationed in the Philippines. As it majored on subjects that would help men talk to their batmen, it was of limited use. The phrase that stuck most readily was, "Where are the underpants?"

From the day their ship docked at Manila, Norman plunged into work at the OMF Publishers. The Pub, as it was dubbed locally, was then situated on United Nations Avenue, a very busy thoroughfare. Norman had to leave for work at crack of dawn each day to avoid the possibility of stewing for hours in a traffic jam.

There was so much to learn. As usual he attempted to do it all at once and, accordingly, often felt ill with strain. *Well, it's only for a year*, he would console himself.

In this he was mistaken. The temporary replacement for missionaries on furlough turned out to be a permanent appointment, and Norman was eventually to be manager of the Pub for seven years. Fortunately, he had no idea of this in 1958 or he might have folded up with fright.

Another OMFer, Maurine Flowers, was to say, "I've learned throughout the years that a genuine realization of personal inadequacy is my biggest asset *provided* it is kept coupled with faith's appropriation of God's total sufficiency." This was Norman's experience also, and the new responsibilities in Manila threw him into even greater dependence upon God than ever before.

OMF Publishers, as its name implied, was not just a retail bookstore. Because of import restrictions and the high cost of foreign materials, one of the aims of OMF in the Philippines was to produce good literature locally and cheaply. This not only meant reprinting many English language books, but also producing tracts, picture strip books and other literature in the main local languages. Norman had no previous experience of the mechanics of publishing, but soon realized that it was imperative that he understand the whole process thoroughly.

The Pub did not run its own presses, but contracted work out to commercial printers. Carelessness and corner-cutting on the part of contractors sometimes resulted in serious mistakes and loss of valuable stock. Close supervision was essential. Sometimes Norman found himself spending days at a time shuttling between printers just checking for errors and ensuring that a reasonable standard of production was maintained.

"It's a funny thing about a secular printing press," he said once. "It will print millions of sample ballot papers for election-campaigning without a hitch. But put on a Christian tract, and suddenly things start to go wrong with that press. This or that catches, and paper is wasted; ink is mixed badly and the shade is wrong; even the type gets muddled."

There was an instance, when printing the English version of a tract, that the vital word "sins" was altered (after the third and final proofreading!) to another word which made nonsense of the message. Norman was never sure that this alteration hadn't been made by someone with malicious intent. Twenty thousand copies were run off before he discovered the mistake. One young lady in that firm will never forget the word "sins" as she had to stick it over the error in every copy! In another booklet, *One Hundred Questions on the Christian Life*, the Lord's name was altered for no apparent reason.

The printing and distribution of Christian literature was warfare against the Evil One, every step of the way. Frequently, the call went out to prayer partners to cover a particular printing through the press. At the Pub, they were producing large quantities of material. In one typical year 52 items of new literature were published.

Probably the most successful publication during these years was a pictorial *Life of Christ* in colour. This attractive booklet sold hundreds of thousands of copies in several languages throughout the Philippines and in other South East Asian countries as well. Norman used to get quite lyrical about this production. Its cartoon strip presentation of the gospel story was not only appealing but could be read and understood by the millions of Filipinos who were classified as limited literates.

Paper for these publications was expensive and always hard to come by. At any one time there was a long list of manuscripts waiting to be processed. The team at the Pub was constantly in prayer about this recurring need.

On one occasion, Norman got wind of a large quantity of surplus paper that was being disposed of at the US Naval Base. He joined the scramble to procure some. With a sinking heart, he heard the price that was being asked. There wasn't that much money available.

"Lord," he prayed silently, "You know how badly we need that paper."

Then, feeling somewhat embarrassed, he tendered for a portion of the paper, naming a price that was twenty percent less than the quote.

How it happened, he doesn't quite know, but he got the lot! When later he went to pay for it, he received another surprise. The Christian servicemen on the Base had footed the bill, and also the cost of transport to Manila. What unlooked for provision! Two tons of high grade paper was enough to publish the Scripture Union Notes for several years, and other things besides.

One of the first projects Norman had floated at the Pub was the production and distribution of the Scripture Union Bible Reading Card. To get people reading the Bible regularly was always a priority with him. Daily, systematic Bible reading had been the foundation of his own Christian life, and he had found the SU Bible reading programme and method most helpful to him through the years in maintaining a meaningful devotional time.

He had been instrumental in getting Scripture Union off the ground in Singapore and in Malaysia. Now he set about selling it to the Philippines. At first only the cards were printed, in all the primary languages. They gave the Bible reading for each day along with instruction on how to read in order to understand and benefit from what was read.

It was quite some time before the Scripture Union Bible Reading Notes could also be prepared and printed, but eventually these too were made available. Amy rewrote the Notes into basic English to aid the Tagalog translator. By the third year, when Alethe Clezy, the first Scripture Union worker, was appointed to the Philippines, there were already five hundred regular subscribers to the Bible Reading Notes. The organization continued to expand until, a few years later, the first Filipino national, Dr Val Magalit, was appointed to head up the work.

Early on in his time at the Pub, Norman discovered that it is easier to produce Christian literature than it is to get rid of it. Distribution is always the bottleneck.

What use are all these books piled up in the stockroom? he worried. *We must find a better method of distribution that we have now.*

Manila is a huge city but, from the beginning, Norman's vision was to see OMF Publishers reach out beyond the city to make Christian literature available throughout the nation. How was this to be achieved?

As in Malaya, he started by purchasing a van for outstation trips. The prophets of doom foretold disaster. "For one thing," they said, "the roads are too dangerous. This is not Malaya." Just the goad needed for a stubborn old Scot! He pushed through the opposition and soon the "far and wide" trips began. Sometimes Amy accompanied him, other times he went with a Filipino staff member.

Not only did they sell literature directly, but they sold the "idea" of literature. People were challenged to use it in ministry and carefully instructed on how to obtain supplies. Purchasing anything by mail was a difficult procedure for most people.

When Norman arrived in one remote area, the rice harvest was in full swing. The handful of Christians to whom he spoke decided to launch out and buy tracts to distribute to the reapers. For, as one man put it, "We want to harvest men for Christ!"

In another town, Norman challenged a young Christian who ran a news stand on a busy street corner.

"You sell newspapers and cigarettes. How about selling some books about Jesus as well? This way you can serve Him and tell others about the Saviour too."

"But I am a very poor man. Books are expensive and people don't read much," was the reply.

"Look at these," said Norman, taking out copies of the *Life of Christ* and other cartoon strip books. The man's eyes brightened. They shouldn't be hard to sell! After all, the

Filipinos were interested in religion. Comic books were his best sellers too and these attractive booklets were comparable in price.

"Well," he agreed cautiously, "I might be able to put up a few pesos. I would like to tell others about the Lord Jesus."

Many people cooked and sold food for a living. "Invest in eternal life," Norman would urge Christian hawkers. "Get some tracts and give them out along with the bowls of rice and bottles of pop you sell. Say something like this, 'You are buying food for your body. I want to give you also food for your soul.'"

In practical ways like this, Norman and his colleagues encouraged Christians everywhere to use literature for evangelism. In addition to this, they tried to find a church or a Christian businessman in each main centre who would be willing to set up a larger outlet for Christian books.

There were many heartaches and disappointments. Sometimes it was necessary to help an outlet get established by making an initial gift of stock. People got enthused and meant well, but funds would be corrupted and debts go unpaid. Poverty and inexperience were the usual reasons why outlets failed.

However, in spite these setbacks, the next few years saw the establishment of more than fifty outlets for the sale and distribution of Christian literature. Norman's vision to see this material made available throughout the land was becoming a reality.

Most of the literature was sown by faith and the sowers rarely learned of the results. Now and again, however, they did hear a story that mightily encouraged them in their efforts.

One of the team at the Pub, Pag-asa, bought a supply of gospel tracts for distribution. On the back of every one she carefully wrote her name and address. In his promotion talks, Norman stressed that this should be done. How else would an inquirer know where to turn for further help? What fisherman would throw his baited hook into the sea and not have it firmly attached to line and rod?

Pag-asa's younger sister, also a committed Christian, "borrowed" some of these tracts one day. On her way to high school, she passed City Hall where a number of sorry-looking prisoners were awaiting trial.

"May I give these men something to read?" she asked the guard. He agreed, and she gave each man a tract.

Some days later, a letter arrived at the store for Pag-asa. It was beautifully written, and the writer inquired if he could learn more about the message in the tract. He was one of the convicts who had been at City Hall, and was in Manila's main jail. How that man was prayed for at the daily staff prayer sessions!

At Pag-asa's request, two OMF men went to the prison and met this inquirer. They told of the Lord's power to save anyone who trusted in Him. It "happened" that this was the only time they could have talked with him. The very next day, he was sent with a batch of other prisoners to a penal farm in the far south of the Philippines.

Months later, when Norman was in the southern island of Mindanao, he checked on this man and found that, although still a prisoner and living in the most disheartening surroundings, he was witnessing brightly for Christ.

As the whole operation grew and developed, Norman's own promotional thrust shifted to literature workshops. He was becoming well known and received many invitations to run workshops and seminars for key groups of people such as pastors, missionaries and Bible Society colporteurs.

His emphasis was always on distribution. As Clarence Jones of the Christian radio station HCJB said when visiting the Philippines, "God has given us the Bread. He doesn't want bakers. He wants delivery boys!"

Norman was one of God's delivery boys. Not only did he deliver the Bread through literature, but he delivered it through preaching. He loved to preach. At the same time, he was conscious that to preach to others was a solemn responsibility. The Lord had anointed His servant with unusual persuasive power and his hearers were moved to transact business with God.

Norman poured out his heart and his life in his sermons. "I want to tell you today about the Lord, my Saviour, who has delivered my soul from death, my eyes from tears and my feet from stumbling" (Psalm 116:8). Everywhere there was great hunger for Bible exposition and invitations came from all directions for him to preach the Word. A wide conference ministry developed.

Where he preached, he always took books. Let the written word reinforce the spoken word. "I'd just as soon sell a good Christian book as preach a sermon!" he claimed, and did both with equal fervour.

One of the most challenging ministries with which Norman became involved was the Overseas Christian Servicemen's Centers (OCSC) in the Philippines. He was often requested to preach at special meetings and conferences for men and women of the American armed forces. Later he was asked to be one of an advisory committee of three senior men to help OCSC younger workers in their service.

The Vietnam war was in full spate at the time, and men and women were coming all the time into Camp John Hay at Baguio for rest and recreation. On a number of occasions, Norman was called on to speak there.

Weekends often found the Macs at Clark Air Base or Subic Bay Naval Base or both for ministry. Every time they stepped through the entrance, they were in the USA! But sadly, just outside the base limits were parasite cities where vice and evil flourished. Nightclubs and brothels catered to the worst instincts of the servicemen. Thousands of young fellows destroyed themselves in these places, but scores were wonderfully salvaged from the very gates of hell by the work of the OCSC. Norman personally had the joy of leading many to the Saviour.

At one conference at Subic Bay, he gave a very solemn message to the fellows. They parted, saying they'd see each other next day. But, at three in the morning, all were called out to take their battleship to Vietnam, and Norman did not meet many of them again.

A young man and his wife who came to know Christ at Clark Air Base were Ben and Jane Draper. Little did any of them dream then that this couple would later join OMF and Ben would become Director of the work in Taiwan.

Perhaps, for Norman personally, the high spot in his conference ministry was reached in 1968 when he was invited to be main speaker at the Inter-Varsity Fellowship Conference in New Zealand. He, who had not been past third year at high school and had carried through life an inferiority complex about his own academic ability, was to bring God's message to university students from all over the country. What a far cry from the young farm labourer who had knelt to yield to the Lord in a shepherd's hut 37 years before!

As he looked at the rows of expectant young faces turned towards him, he was deeply moved. "Oh God," he asked silently, "who am I that you should have elevated me to such a place of leadership and influence?"

"I chose you," came the answer. "It is I who took you from the pasture, from following the sheep, in order that you should be prince (messenger) to my people Israel" (2 Samuel 7:8). Even as Norman began to preach with authority and power, his grateful heart was bowed down before his Master in humble adoration.

People showed their appreciation for his ministry in many ways. At a rural conference in the Philippines, a man brought him a little present clutched in a paper bag. It was an apple. The speaker, very touched, could only guess what sacrifices the man had made to pay for this treasure from Japan.

In a message elsewhere, Norman referred to how English people like him enjoyed a cup of tea. Next day, his Filipina hostess presented him with a glass of hot, milkless, sugarless tea, and the whole world seemed to stop as with great gusto, he drank it down!

The promotional aspect of the literature work was meat and drink to Norman. His enthusiasm for getting the message out was unquenchable and he revelled in the privilege he had of being part of this vital service.

"I wouldn't be anywhere else in the world," he exulted, "and my heart is full of thanksgiving day by day as I see literature going out from this place."

At the same time, however, he fought some private battles. He wasn't altogether happy at the Pub. The problem was that, while he had spiritual gifts of leadership, he was decidedly weak in administrative ability and knew it. Through his enthusiastic, inspirational leadership and sheer hard work, the Pub had expanded into a big, complex operation, but its organization and day-to-day administration was a millstone around his neck. When he finally left the Publishers, the book selling and publishing departments had to be separated, each with its own manager.

Committee meetings, which inevitably multiply like barnacles on a growing business, irked him terribly. While genuinely appreciative of the more analytical capacity display-ed by others, his own instinctive reaction was an impatient, *Oh, let's stop talking about it and get on and do it!* While this impetuousness may have led to premature action at times, and certainly resulted in much unnecessary expenditure of energy, it also meant that a tremendous amount was actually accomplished.

Norman found it hard to delegate and, consequently, took more and more of the load on himself and consistently overworked. He was always anxious not to ask the staff to do anything that he was unprepared to do himself. But his "too quick" assistance was sometimes interpreted as interference or implied criticism. A hard-driving, meticulous worker himself, he expected others to be the same, and didn't always made enough allowance for differences in temperament and work patterns. Perhaps it was the young OMF men in the Pub who took the brunt of this as Norman was, naturally, more understanding and patient with national workers who seemed not to be performing well. He expected more of the other missionaries.

"He can be so critical," complained one young missionary colleague.

While Norman had a genuine concern for the well-being of all his staff, he was an incurable activist and not naturally a good listener. This also led to some misunderstandings on his part and resentments on the part of others.

That these weaknesses didn't cause serious rifts in the ranks was largely due to the fact that Norman was utterly sincere in his dealings with the staff and they realized it. When occasion demanded it, he was always ready to say, "I'm sorry." He truly loved them and they knew that they could count on his support if they got into trouble.

Several times, due to inexperience or errors in judgment, staff members were responsible for large financial losses. In such cases, the boss never ripped them off, and his understanding, "Never mind, we all make mistakes," bound his people to him. For these things they loved him and willingly forgave him his shortcomings.

However, he himself worried over them incessantly, and time and again would dearly love to have run away from it all. *Oh, if only I had just one particular job to do, and didn't have to be responsible for the whole boiling!* he would think wistfully. But "can't" had been buried years ago. The Master had called him to this task, so the response of true faith had to be, "I can do all things through Christ who strengthens me" (Phil 4:13).

Initially, Norman had been very lonely. One of the penalties of growing older is that most of one's fellow workers get younger and are taken up with different interests. This was so at the Pub. Norman longed for a congenial friend in Manila as he'd had in other places. The Lord lovingly gave him his desire when, quite early on, the Macs met Dr Ed and Helen Spahr who were in the same age group as themselves. The Spahrs were co-founders of Grace Christian High School and Ed was also pastor of Grace Bible Church. Immediately Norman was knit to this brother who also loved his Lord and served him with a whole heart. They enjoyed deep, satisfying fellowship in spiritual things and their friendship was a tremendous strength to Norman through many crises.

Although the Macs didn't realize it, the rich, full years in the Philippines were drawing to a close. Throughout these years, Singapore had developed into a major Asian metropolis, geographically and economically strategic for the whole area. The church there was also mushrooming. It was high time that a strong base be established in the city for the distribution of evangelical Christian literature.

By 1968, when the Macs went on furlough, the situation which had prevented OMF proceeding with this plan ten years earlier had been resolved. A request went to Norman from headquarters. "Would you consider coming to Singapore to establish a Christian bookstore under the auspices of the Scripture Union?"

This was a complete surprise, but it touched an old chord. Immediately the Spirit confirmed in his heart that this call was from Him. The time was ripe now for the fulfilment of his original vision.

By the time the Macs arrived in Singapore, Norman's mind was seething with plans. How he'd longed for a challenge like this! Before their bags were unpacked, he was off down town to assess the situation.

His total assets were a desk, a few thousand dollars worth of stock (some of it very shabby) and two Chinese sales girls inherited from the old Christian Bookroom.

The goal was a bright, modern retail store and a wholesale department which would be capable of supplying the needs of many small retailers throughout the Singapore and Malaysian region.

I'm going to need experienced help, he thought. *Who can we ask?*

Suddenly, he thought of me. Failing to get into Indonesia as a missionary with OMF, I had been working for the past four years at the Evangel Book Centre in Kuala Lumpur. What a joy it would be to have his own daughter as a fellow-worker! But the pundits advised against it. Even the beloved and understanding director, Mr Arnold Lea, said kindly, "Norman, it never works!"

However, I was experienced and available. If I hadn't been a daughter, I'd have been the obvious one to call. Eventually, it was agreed to give it a try.

It did work! It worked marvellously for both of us, and we enjoyed, in perfect harmony, some of our happiest years in the Lord's service.

After a few initial hassles, the SU Christian Book Centre expanded rapidly. The staff grew from four to eight and the Lord bonded us into a great team.

Dad's enthusiasm for the work and devotion to the Lord were contagious. He loved his staff and was loved in return. "Come on folks, we've a job to do!" was his rallying cry. He led by example. If he worked us all to exhaustion, he did the same himself. Wherever the action was, he would be there in the middle of it.

His energy seemed boundless. Only Mother and I ever saw him lie grey and groaning with angina pains and worried that he might suddenly drop dead in his tracks. No amount of nagging on our part would stop him lifting heavy boxes of books and generally overdoing it.

"I'd rather wear out than rust out," he'd retort when we remonstrated with him.

Within two years, the SU Christian Book Centre became a flourishing business with retail and wholesale departments and a national manager in training. It was another success story, result of the right man in the right place at the right time.

One day I had reason to see our director, Mr Lea. Unexpectedly, he asked, "How is it that Norman is so successful in everything he does? What is his spiritual secret? Is it prayer?"

"No," I replied doubtfully. "He prays earnestly and is zealous about prayer, but I don't think it's that."

"Is it faith?"

"I don't think so. In fact, his natural tendency is to worry. I believe he has quite a struggle for faith."

"What is it then?"

I fumbled uncertainly for the answer at the time, but have since given the matter considerable reflection.

Dad has tremendous drive and commitment, coupled with natural ability and unusual physical stamina. All this energy would have made him prosper in any career he took up. But the intense purpose and strength of his life has been harnessed solely to the Lord's interests, not his own.

If Mr Lea were to ask me that question again, I would answer, "Norman's spiritual secret of success is selflessness. He is selfless in his relation to God and unselfish in his relation to men. He always puts his own concerns last."

Perhaps the thing that most disappoints him in others is what appears to be half-hearted commitment or self-interested service. He just can't understand tepidness in the Lord's servants.

Dad's energetic promotional work throughout the city eventually earned him the nickname, "Mr Literature!" People used this appellation affectionately or teasingly. I could imagine the Master using it another way.

"Well done, Mr Literature, good and faithful servant!"

CHAPTER 14

LOAVES AND FISHES

When the Macs had first arrived in Manila in 1958, Amy was decidedly lost. Her last child was about to leave the nest. Lesley, at six years old, would be going to Chefoo School in Baguio. Years before, a missionary with an only child had said, "It's all very well for you. If anything happens to one of your children, you've got more!"

That's one way of looking at it, I suppose, thought Amy. *But having more children not only multiplies one's joys, it also multiplies one's responsibilities, even possibly one's sorrows, and certainly occupies one's time.*

Amy had no burning ambition to have a career of her own. Although, technically, she had full missionary status in the mission, she had accepted the reality that her role was primarily that of wife and mother. Occasionally there would be tension between what she felt was expected of her as a missionary and what she knew were the needs of her family, but this was never an acute problem. In the early years, the Lord gave her "missionary work" to do that was compatible with her "home ministry."

Parting with Lesley was especially painful, however. Not only was she the youngest but, being six years behind Twink, she had been like an only child for quite a while. Now, with neither chick nor child, what was a bereft mother to do with her empty days?

It was ironical that, just as Norman was reaching full-stride in his literature ministry and experiencing more fulfilment than ever before in his life, she should suddenly be left in limbo.

"Lord, what am *I* going to do?" she prayed. "Have you any particular work assigned for *me*?"

In her early years as a missionary, there had been scant opportunity to develop her special gifts and abilities in music, teaching and writing. Her energies had, perforce, been spent in caring for little children and in serving the practical needs of fellow workers.

Regretfully, she thought of her music. Was it too late to revive her expertise in this area? The Filipinos were such musical people.

One of the greatest personal deprivations of missionary life for her, especially in China days, was not to be within miles of a piano for years at a time. When she came across one, it was pure joy to sit down and play it. Except, perhaps, on one memorable occasion.

During a rural conference in the Philippines some time later, an elderly man asked the Macs if they could possibly spare time to visit in his home which was nearby. It wasn't easy to fit in but they made the effort.

They ascended the steps of his thatched house and were shown into the main room with its scrupulously polished wooden floor from which every speck of dust had been lovingly removed. To their amazement, the Macs saw a piano in one corner. The instrument was old and battered, but still, a piano. Their host was obviously very proud of this show piece and related how it had been hidden away during the Japanese occupation. But now it faced his guests in all its ancient glory.

As they all sat down, their host gave a lordly wave towards the instrument and said, "Play something, play something!" He unearthed an old hymnbook minus cover and with its edges gnawed by white ants. Finally, between them, they succeeded in finding a whole page of music.

Realizing that this was an auspicious occasion and desiring to please their host, Amy made a suitable fuss of arranging herself on the stool and the music on the stand. Then, with a flourish, she began. At the first chord, the whole front of the piano collapsed into her lap. She sat there in stunned silence.

Gently across the room came two words from their host, "H'm, defective!"

Amy wasn't sure if he meant the piano or the pianist and didn't dare look at Norman. Together, they pushed things into precarious place once more and retired to the other side of the room to recuperate on cold drinks and biscuits. If ever there was a lost chord that was it!

Although, in more recent years, Amy was often asked to play the piano at meetings and to sing an occasional solo, she realized that she was no longer equipped for a major music ministry.

But there was writing, and she loved to write. *Should I work on another book?* she wondered. *But about what?*

While her expertise in music had withered, her talent as a writer had grown. This was largely due to a very positive attitude towards life. There was, she believed, something to be learned from every situation, good or bad.

She had an unquenchable thirst for knowledge, read widely and enjoyed thoughtful conversation. With her inquiring mind and observant eye, she studied the people and things around her wherever she went. Over the years she amassed an amazing amount of information. A lot of this was kept as jottings in notebooks. A lot more was stored in a very retentive memory.

Mother has a mind like a computer, I've sometimes thought. *Press the right buttons and it will throw up data on a wide assortment of subjects. What you get will be detailed and usually accurate.*

What Amy discovered, she wrote about. Her efforts were never mere exercises in self-expression nor simply creative compositions. She was a missionary with a message to proclaim and, in all her writing, she sought to fulfil this purpose.

The net result of all this was that she did not go to seed in often unstimulating surroundings and unconducive circumstances. On the contrary, these very things became grist to the mill of experience which widened her horizons and nurtured her intellect. What she wrote was also widely used to promote interest and prayer support for the mission and its various ministries.

The answer to Amy's request, "What shall I do?" came sooner than she expected. Before the Macs had been in Manila 24 hours, she was asked to write a radio script for the Far East Broadcasting Company (FEBC). Her first reaction was a cautious, "Let me pray about it for a while. I hadn't thought about doing this sort of thing." But, as there was an urgent deadline to meet, she ended up writing the script while sitting on their unpacked baggage.

In the will of the Lord, this triggered off a longterm radio ministry which extended to a weekly programme for six years and a second programme to the South Pacific for three years. When it was discovered that she had an excellent broadcasting voice, Amy was required not only to write the programmes, but also to deliver them in person.

Life is full of surprises, and this was one of them. As a young teacher, she had broadcast to schools in New Zealand, but had never thought to do such work again. When, later, in their little shack in Gemas Bahru, the Macs had listened to their first programme from FEBC, Manila, it never crossed Amy's mind that one day the Lord would use her personally in this special kind of outreach.

The next request to come her way was to teach at the Far Eastern Bible Institute and Seminary.

"Yes, Lord," she responded eagerly. "You know how I love to teach!"

Along with two Bible subjects, she had to compile (from scratch!) a new course in Christian Journalism and Writing. Teaching *and* writing? Her two loves combined! With a grateful heart she received her new job description.

This too developed into a longterm ministry of teaching

which was a great joy to her. Physically, though, she found it very arduous because, aside from the hours of preparation in the heat, it involved a couple of hours' travel through Manila's chaotic traffic twice weekly to lecture for three hours at a stretch. According to her, the astronauts who walk in space have an easier time than those who brave Manila's highways.

She would travel by jeepney, the incredible local equivalent of a mini-bus, open back and sides. These vehicles are usually gaudily painted, fitted with all kinds of gadgets and artistic or religious extras and are often their owners' pride and joy. One suspects that more attention is given to their outward appearance than to their inward parts, and journeys by jeepney can be quite terrifying, especially when taken at their usual breakneck speed through heavy traffic.

Norman and Amy were careering madly along in a jeepney one night, just missing everything by a hair's breadth, when they happened to look up and notice a motto painted on the roof above their heads. It simply said, "*God bless us all*". To which they added a devout "Amen!"

As Amy laboured over the preparation of the first course on Christian writing and then taught it to a class of three "guinea pigs," she had no idea that, in God's plan, she was laying the foundation for something much bigger.

The first premonition of this came at the OMF missionary conference in Baguio in 1960 when she received a clear directive from the Lord, "Offer this course by correspondence."

She was jolted by this unexpected development and shrank from all that it would involve. It meant not only preparing detailed lessons and marking many extra assignments, but also attending to the business side of things. Business was definitely not her forte.

It wasn't possible to evade such clear leading, however. She choked back her initial negative reaction, and reminded herself sternly that "can't" must remain buried. "All right, Lord," she agreed, "I'll do it."

The Christian Writers' Course (CWC) by correspondence was launched at the beginning of July that year. Within two months, dozens of people had enrolled from all walks of life, all keen to serve the Master by writing. At first the course was made available only for people in the Philippines. Its primary purpose was to train indigenous writers, nationals who could present the Christian message with cultural appeal and relevance for their own people.

But soon, inquiries started to pour in from overseas. Apparently, with self-conscious nationalism on the rise all through the Third World, the need for indigenous writers was more widespread than just the Philippines.

In the next few years, CWC went international and eventually trained students from fifty countries. This was no planned effort to enter the field of training — at least not on the human level. The work of the CWC developed so quickly, Amy was soon running to keep up!

She knew her life to be unspeakably enriched through personal interaction with her international students. Only committed Christians "who had something to say" spiritually, were accepted for training. Many had deep and wonderful experiences of the Lord. Many struggled to write in English which was their second language.

A university student described a crowded jeep ride. "There were six of us all mystically united in aromatic perspiration." Such flowery writing, of which there was plenty, needed to be pruned of its verbiage.

"Give it to us quickly," demands Twentieth Century Man, "or we can't be bothered reading it!"

"Cut down and simplify," was the comment Amy wrote most frequently on her students' manuscripts.

The numbers who sought training soon became too great to handle from Amy's office. Inevitably there had to be decentralization and, in several countries, missions and Bible schools asked to have and adapt the Course for their particular use. This the OMF gladly allowed, for the vision was for national writers everywhere.

A rather humorous incident occurred when a man in the Philippines wrote to an overseas Bible School about a Christian Writers' Course they were offering. They referred him back to Amy (as it was the OMF's Course they had permission to use!). But he was not interested in taking instruction at close quarters. Distance lends enchantment!

As their ministries grew and gathered momentum, both the Macs began to feel endlessly exhausted in the heat and humidity of Manila. Temperatures were often in the upper nineties day and night. How long could they keep going like this? It was getting them down.

The Tarkingtons, staff workers with the Overseas Christian Servicemen's Centers, were kind enough to be concerned about this and said they were praying that the Macs could get an air-conditioner. The Macs weren't. How could they ask the Lord for such a luxury?

A while later, the Tarkingtons turned up with one they insisted was not being used. It was fitted into the bedroom and both Norman and Amy started to sleep as they had not done for months. Then they discovered that many people in Manila used air-conditioners. As one missionary reasoned, "If the Lord had sent me to Alaska, He'd have supplied a stove to keep me warm. So now I'm in the tropics, I've got to keep cool!"

One of their concerns was the running cost. Was it right to incur such expense?

They were in fear and trembling waiting for the first electricity bill. A few minutes before the man came to read the meter they received a letter from a serviceman in the USA who had previously been stationed in the Philippines. In it was US$25 "towards an air-conditioner!"

"You could have bowled us over with a feather," Amy told her mother. What perfect timing. How they thanked the Lord for this loving provision.

Immediately, their work output increased fifty percent and, even more important, they had fresh inspiration to get on with the job.

In addition to their busy schedules, Norman and Amy entertained a constant flow of visitors, many from overseas. Most were a pleasure, some were a pain.

One time, when they had been asked to meet somebody's relatives, and had entertained them all through the long, hot day, they mentioned that their church was putting on a special cantata that evening. Filipinos are beautiful singers. Would the couple care to attend? No thank you, they had planned to do a tour of the city's night clubs!

1 Corinthians 15:58 came with comfort and undergirding on such occasions, "You know that nothing you do in the Lord's service is ever useless."

One memorable visit was that of Kyoshi Iwai. Norman and Amy had been asked to meet this young Japanese student who would be passing through Manila en route to Japan after a course of study at Moore Theological College in Sydney.

They met him on board ship to take him ashore for the day. But first, he pulled a piece of paper out of his pocket.

"This," he said, "is the name of a Filipino pastor my father wants me to look up. They knew each other during the War."

On arrival at the house, the Macs started a telephone search for the pastor, and eventually located him living on the outskirts of Manila. Shortly after, they were knocking on his door. The old man opened it himself. He had recently undergone an operation for cataracts, so did not see his visitors very clearly.

"Pastor," they began, "this is Kyoshi Iwai. His father knew you in the War." The pastor was dumbfounded.

"Iwai?" he gasped. "Iwai? He was my friend! Come in, come in!" He led them into an inner room. There on the wall hung a large framed photograph of a high-ranking Japanese officer.

"My father!" exclaimed Kyoshi. He stepped up to the picture to read the typed text which had been stuck under it. "Jesus said, I say unto you, I have not found so great faith, no, not in Israel."

Deep emotions were stirred as Pastor told his story.

During the Japanese occupation of the Philippines, their little group of Christians met regularly for worship. This officer started to attend the services and was, not unnaturally, treated with a great deal of suspicion. However, he always removed his military hat and hung it in the church porch before going in to kneel humbly in prayer with the other worshippers. He gradually won their confidence, studied Tagalog, and actually preached in that language.

"I have the notes of his first sermon," Pastor told Kyoshi with delight. He used to buy Bibles and sell them cheaply to those who needed them, and then use the proceeds to buy more.

"He was a man of great faith," said Pastor. He mused for a few moments, then continued, "We broke bread together. He was my true friend."

The Macs found it tremendously moving to picture the scene, as both men knelt together at the foot of the Cross, enjoying that fellowship that can only be found in Christ, whatever the circumstances.

"I will honour those who honour Me," promised the Lord in 1 Samuel 3:30. Colonel Iwai had honoured God, and on his return to Japan, God had fulfilled His promise. Iwai resigned from the Army and entered into training for the ministry. God honoured him also by calling three of his sons into full-time Christian service. Two served in Japan, another went to represent Scripture Union in Indonesia.

Pastor also knew God's blessing in his home and family life, so vital in the Philippines. When Norman and Amy met him, he had 108 living descendants. He was later to prepare a Ministers' Manual, which OMF Publishers printed for use throughout the land.

Soon after this, the Macs went on furlough for a year and the CWC was left in the capable hands of Ralph Toliver, an OMFer who was a journalist and writer. When they returned, Amy wondered if she should leave the course with him and devote herself to other forms of writing.

Again the Lord spoke clearly, "See to it that *you* complete the work *you* have received in the Lord" (Colossians 4:17). So Amy took up the reins once more.

Early in 1964, she had to undergo major surgery. It is customary in many Asian hospitals for a relative to accompany the patient right into the ward and to help with the general nursing, and sometimes even to prepare food. I was a new missionary then, held up in Singapore awaiting my visa to Indonesia. Because I was free and Mother would need nursing for some weeks after the operation, the mission leaders suggested I go and care for her, a very nice bonus for the three of us.

Years later, Twink was in Manorom Christian Hospital in Thailand for the birth of her baby. She wrote to Mother in mock rebuke, "Where were you? There was a granny under every bed except mine!"

Convalescence for Amy took longer than expected. A Wycliffe missionary kindly donated a pint of blood for a transfusion, which prompted an OMFer to quip, "Wycliffe blood, eh? Now you'll be translated!"

Whether the extra boost given by the Wycliffe blood was responsible or not, Amy launched out immediately after this and prepared an advanced course for CWC graduates. It was a specialized study in writing Christian fiction, a difficult subject for most people. As numbers wanting this course were never large, it was not offered by correspondence.

In the same year, another significant new development took place, due primarily to the vision of Alfred and May Johnston. They arranged a ten-day workshop in Davao City for 24 prospective writers at which Amy was asked to teach.

All was going well when, suddenly, fire broke out in the business section of the city, which eventually gutted several blocks. The flames stopped just short of the large wooden building in which they were holding the workshop. Everyone pitched in to evacuate the stock from the Christian Bookstore. Gangs of helpers carried books down the road to a large stone church. Among the helpers were half a dozen or so small boys about nine years of age. They were indefatigable.

After their hot journeys, running and fetching, Amy offered each of them a bottle of pop. They were adamant in their refusal. "No, Ma'am, you musn't spend your money on us, we're all right." How different from the hordes of looters who swarmed over the ruins. These youngsters went to a Christian school!

The workshop students had firsthand experience in producing news stories about the fire in which they been involved. Later, they were all invited to a meal with Dr and Mrs Lim, a godly couple and friends of all the Lord's people. Mrs Lim's seventy-year-old parents had lost everything in the fire, "except His peace," she said. When the flames got close, the old man had calmly taken his wife by the arm and said, "Come on." They'd picked up their Bibles and walked out.

Some very useful material for publication was produced by these Davao writers, including a tract for students that was widely used.

This first workshop was followed by many more throughout the Philippines. They were always strenuous occasions. "I'll be a good writer — or burst!" exclaimed a would-be author at one of them, summing up what many of her perspiring companions were feeling.

Perhaps the high point for Amy in this most satisfying work was when she was asked to take a course on advanced Christian writing in Taiwan. It was attended by about forty participants, winners of various writing competitions, and editors, some highly qualified. She had the lion's share of the lectures. Others, being specialists, had one lecture each! Privately she was amazed that, lacking any formal training in journalism herself, she should be there at all, *and* be regarded as an "expert"!

A personal touch was to discover that one of the older men at the workshop had been in Chengdu when she and Norman were married. Back in Sichuan days, Douglas Sargent had urged this young Nationalist soldier to accept the Lord, but to no avail. After he retreated to Taiwan, however, he did become a keen Christian, and had won one of the writing contests that qualified him to attend this workshop.

Amy was unable to do as much personal writing in these years of training others as she might otherwise have done. There were two notable exceptions.

The first was a novel on the Philippines which was rejected by the publishers! This was a severe disappointment. *And how humiliating for a teacher of writing*, she thought ruefully. *Probably sent to keep me humble, in fact.* Sadly, she leafed through the manuscript. It represented so much hard labour. She was about to bury it in the bottom of the filing cabinet when, suddenly, she changed her mind. Cremation would be more decisive!

The other was the biography of a fellow worker which was published in England by Marshall, Morgan and Scott. On 9 May 1963, the Macs were shocked by the news that May Roy had been killed in an overturned jeep. She was a missionary to the tribal people of Mindoro, Philippines. General Director, J O Sanders, asked Amy to write the story of this outstanding pioneer who had been not only a fellow-New Zealander but a close personal friend. It was a sad assignment. Amy prayed that she would be able to portray May's life in such a way that young believers who read it would be inspired to give their lives to the Lord as totally as she had done.

The Christian Writers' Course went with Amy to Singapore. In spite of decentralization, there were still many students enrolled with her. During these three years, she also conducted writers' workshops in other places including Indonesia, Thailand, Malaysia and New Zealand. A new emphasis was the training of national script writers for radio programmes. With an estimated fifty million radios in Asia, Christian broadcasting stations were having a fruitful ministry but were always crying out for good quality material.

As Amy saw her graduates appearing in print and taking up responsible editorial positions with Christian publishers, she was deeply grateful.

"It's just like the miracle of the loaves and fishes," she often marvelled. "All I had was a small talent. Yet, in God's hands, it has been multiplied a thousandfold. What a Master to serve!"

Just before the Macs finally left Asia, Amy was surprised to receive a handsome plaque, awarded by Evangelical Literature Overseas. The inscription read, "For the spirit of dedication shown in the encouragement and guidance of national Christian writers and editors, and for diligent research into the development of educational programmes for such training."

Amy never hung this trophy. She knew, better than anyone, that the success of the Christian Writers' Course was due, not to her own astute planning and expertise, but to the Lord's direction and blessing.

CHAPTER 15

THE CROWNING YEARS

On 1 October 1969, the Mac's long-time friend and counsellor, Mr J Oswald Sanders, retired as General Director of the OMF. The torch was handed on to Dr Michael Griffiths. At the dedication ceremony, Mike spoke on "What is the attitude of a man who succeeds another in God's work?" He focused his remarks on Hebrew 13:8. A time of changeover could bring a sense of insecurity, but "Jesus Christ is the same, yesterday, today and forever."

Little did Norman and Amy realize that they would soon be needing this reminder for themselves. God seemed always to be doing the unexpected in their lives. They had known that OMF's Director in New Zealand was due for retirement, but in a vague kind of way also knew that God would supply the man to succeed him.

This vagueness was sharply dispelled one day when Mike called. "Norman," he said, "you know we are looking for a new director in New Zealand. We believe you are the man for the job. Would you be willing?"

Norman was stunned. "But I'm not the man for a job like that!" he exclaimed. In all this happy, busy life in Singapore, he thrived. Mike couldn't really mean him to leave it all and go home to New Zealand. It was unthinkable. The old dislike of administrative work came back in full force. It was too painful to think about, so he tried to shelve the whole question.

One day, about a year later, Mike put his head in the car

window, and asked, "Well, have you bought those tickets to New Zealand yet?" The issue couldn't be dodged any longer.

Then God, always so patient and understanding, spoke gently to his reluctant servant. "I am sending you to New Zealand. You know by now that your disabilities do not disqualify you. You know that I am able to handle all your weaknesses. Think back. Haven't I turned what you thought were stumbling-blocks into stepping stones? I know this is the biggest challenge you have faced yet, but I take full responsibility. Can't you trust Me once more?"

"Yes, Lord," was the hesitant reply "but I confess my heart is heavy."

Amy, too, dreaded the thought of going. Couldn't they finish out their missionary career in Asia? Their lifelong commitment to the Lord and the mission was tested as never before. But after all they had been through with their faithful God, how could they now say "can't."

Norman, in the usual course of events, would have five years until retirement. Mike, in addition to assessing the needs of the work, knew that Norman was physically running himself into the ground, and hoped to prolong his days in a more temperate climate.

This time, when Norman and Amy boarded the plane for the homeland, they knew it was not "au revoir" but "goodbye" — goodbye to the bookstore committee and staff, goodbye to missionary colleagues and goodbye to many other dear friends. Hardest of all was to accept the fact that it was goodbye to Asia. They felt as though their hearts would break.

They flew through the night to Melbourne, arriving there to find the Mission Home closed and the shops shut. It was Queen's Birthday Weekend and folks were away on special assignments. With the temperature fifty degrees lower than in Singapore, the Macs were so cold, inside and out, that they climbed into bed fully dressed. They felt unwelcome and wretched.

Things improved next day as they renewed acquaintance

with friends who invited them to meals and were very kind. Nevertheless, they still felt numb inside and had a sense of walking in unreality.

Their spirits lightened a little as they flew towards the coast of New Zealand's South Island and saw, rising out of the evening mists, the three great snow-capped summits of Cook, Tasman and Sefton. In the light of the setting sun, they glowed with magnificent colour. It was hard to believe that mere man could ever have climbed those remote and shining peaks, but their son Gavin had climbed Mount Cook, the highest, and was preparing to do so again shortly.

The OMF headquarters in New Zealand was in Auckland. Before taking up office, Norman and Amy made a quick trip south to see family members. Their first Sunday in the South they went to a city church, and there the culture shock began! They didn't realize that was what it was, and certainly weren't expecting any such reaction after all the changes they had been through in life.

For years they had lived and worked in countries where populations and churches were largely youthful. The majority of Asia's people are under 25 years of age. So, on this particular Sunday, they thought they'd stumbled on a service for old folks. The choir was mostly older, likewise the congregation, and all were shapeless in thick overcoats and hats (not worn in the tropics). The singing seemed ponderous and lacked the vitality of youth.

The Macs were dismayed. They felt like strangers in their own land. Later, they were to rediscover what they had known on previous furloughs, what warm, generous, caring people were hidden under those coats and hats. It was just that the contrast was too sudden, and too great.

For a long time they felt extremely lonely and insecure. They were themselves older now and it was not easy to break into networks of friendships that had been established for years without them. People were kind and welcoming, but the Macs felt like outsiders, unneeded. They had no place in society. It was a desolate feeling.

The dreadful isolation of many people in western society struck them acutely. They had noticed it before, of course, but this time they were not on furlough, just passing through. They had to be part of it now for the rest of their lives.

When the sun sets in the tropics and the air cools, the people, old and young, spill out on to the streets to eat and socialize. Nobody is alone. There's always someone to talk to. But in New Zealand, especially in winter time, as the sun goes down, doors are closed, blinds pulled and the streets lie empty and cold. Norman and Amy shuddered to think of all the elderly folk and singles shut away from the society of others for long, weary evenings and endless nights. Old age was just around the corner for them too. How could they bear it?

Some tourists who once visited New Zealand were asked, "How was New Zealand?" They replied, "Shut!" The Macs understood what they meant. Shops closed in the evenings, nothing was open all weekend. Asia is never shut. There are always markets and shops open. The cheerful bustle of activity never ceases. To purchase a plastic-wrapped fish fillet from the shelves of a supermarket might be convenient and hygenic, but it doesn't compare in social value with a good-natured haggle over freshness and price with an Asian fishmonger!

In Asia too, they, with their venerable grey heads, were respected by the young who often visited them to socialize or seek advice. But in New Zealand the old are often ignored by the young who seem like a race apart.

The Macs were suffering intense culture shock — in reverse. Sensitive friends, however, realized their emotional difficulties and rallied to their aid. What a tower of strength they were! Among them were Norman's life-long friend Les Rushbrook and Amy's sister Myrle and her husband Stan Conway. Slowly, Norman and Amy began to regain more secure footing in their own country and society.

Undoubtedly, their greatest asset during these difficult days was the presence of Twink, their third daughter, and her husband Bryan Parry. He was a doctor at an Auckland hospital at the time. These two not only gave Norman plenty of encouragement and moral support as he took up his new executive position, but threw their weight energetically into helping him organize OMF youth rallies and they were full of creative ideas for special programmes.

The Parry's first child, Matthew, was born just before the Macs arrived in Auckland and, for an extended period, Norman and Amy had the rare pleasure of being grandparents at close range. To have this little family just around the corner, and never more than a telephone call away, was comfort indeed. Lesley had started nursing training in Auckland too, so they saw her from time to time. Later, she was to become a flight hostess with Air New Zealand and for six-and-a-half years flew on their overseas runs.

For the heavy and far-reaching responsibility of being OMF Director, Norman felt totally and completely inadequate. He came to the job without any overlap or grooming. This, in addition to the strain of cultural readjustment, plus one or two hard knocks from other directions, brought him near to a nervous breakdown for the only time in his life. Also his back played up again and he hobbled around painfully for weeks at a stretch.

"Lord," he cried desperately time and again, "I'm at the end of my tether. This job is too big for me. Help me!" This prayer was answered. Through God's empowering, Norman was able to do the job, not just anyhow, but successfully. He gained the wholehearted cooperation of the staff in the office and the confidence and support of the New Zealand Council.

His enthusiastic representation of OMF throughout the land resulted in thirty new recruits going forward to serve with the Fellowship in Asia. Among these were Twink and Bryan, with two children, destined for Manorom Hospital in Thailand.

Norman's warm relationship with supporters was perhaps his most valuable contribution to OMF. He made a point of visiting or contacting them in person and Amy spent hours writing personal notes to donors. They were made to feel important and appreciated, and their contribution a vital part of the whole mission effort. The family feeling that developed was especially evident at the regional prayer conferences, one of Norman's particular emphases.

Even as the busy years passed, the Macs were aware of a shapeless, grey cloud hovering over the horizon, a cloud they didn't want to see. It was called "retirement." The word has a finality about it that is chilling to an ardent spirit. It suggests leaving the scene of action and withdrawing to a place of seclusion while the rest of the world goes by.

When Norman and Amy returned to New Zealand in 1971, they had found most of their contemporaries diligently pursuing a course called "Preparing for Retirement." This meant buying land lots, building retirement nests, investing money and talking much about the halcyon days ahead. They had felt confused, odd. Here they were, starting on a new, demanding term of service while friends of their age were starting to wind down.

There was nothing they could do about the matter except take a tighter grip on Matthew 6:33 and get on with the job in hand. "Be concerned above everything else with the Kingdom of God, and with what He requires of you, and He will provide you with all these other things."

Inevitably though, as this last term of service passed by, the thought of "What next?" surfaced sharply now and again, threatening to shake their confidence and darken their spirits with doubt. They looked into a blank future. At 65 years of age, they would be released from active service with OMF. They had no home and no place to go.

Psalm 16:8 had been the lodestone of Norman's life for many years, and was now a stimulus to faith. "I have set the Lord always before me. Because He is at my right hand, I shall not be shaken." The Lord had seen them through so many crises. How could He abandon them now? So, as often before in times of danger or want, they expressed their trust by singing John Newton's hymn, "His love in times past forbids me to think he'll leave me at last in trouble to sink."

As their forty nomadic years drew to a close, they started to pray for direction as to where they should "settle." Gradually their thoughts were led to the deep South where Norman had his roots and two sons and their families were then living. It seemed the right general location. But which town? Where, and how?

On Norman's last trip south for OMF, immediately before he was to hand over to John Hewlett, he conducted a series of meetings in Southland and Otago. As he went about, he kept an ear to the ground for any talk of houses, and a mind open to the Lord's choice in the matter.

He was already on his way north again, when he received a long-distance call from Invercargill. "A house came on the market this morning," said a friend excitedly, "but is not yet advertised. We think it could be just what you require. Could you come back and look at it immediately?"

"I'll come right away," was the eager response. As the car sped back over the miles, Norman meditated on the Scripture he had read that very morning. Luke chapter nineteen records a number of cases of incomplete consecration to the Master. Then the Lord seemed to say to him, "You are going to Invercargill to see this house, but remember, whatever you decide, it must be complete consecration still."

As soon as he saw the house, he knew that this was God's place for them! The kind friend who had phoned gave $1,000 to "seal the deal." Another lady did likewise. One couple gave several thousand dollars. In an incredibly short time, God had provided His servants with an ideal home, paid for to the last cent! It was a humbling, yet joyous experience. Hadn't God invited them to trust Him? His promise had never failed in the past. It had not failed now and they rejoiced in His faithfulness.

Now all they had to do was to walk in and settle down. But was it? While packing up to leave Auckland, Amy became all but crippled with excruciating pain in one leg. The doctor said she had damaged a nerve by lifting a too-heavy packing case. No relief came from physiotherapy, so a good deal of time was spent on the horizontal.

Norman left by himself with a car-load of belongings to make the thousand-mile journey south. A few days later, Amy was hoisted into a plane from a wheelchair to go and meet him.

What a thrill to see their home, the first place they could ever call their own. How amazingly good the Lord had been to them — such a comfortable house surrounded by an attractive garden.

But they were not, after all, to live in it for a while. The pain in Amy's leg got no better and she was sent to Dunedin for a month of tests. Finally, when they did return to set up house, Amy was still in great pain. She could work upright for half an hour, and then lie flat for two hours. And so it went on for several months, improvement coming very slowly.

The most immediate need for the Mac's retirement had been for a place to live. Their next concern was for a job to do. They might have retired from the OMF, but they had not retired from the Lord's service. Like the Hebrew slaves who refused to go free when given the opportunity, the cry of both their hearts was, "We love, we love our Master, we will not go out free." Their daily prayer was, and still is, "Lord, give me life till my work is done, and Lord, give me work while my life shall last."

While Amy was still painfully dragging herself around, a long-distance call came from Christchurch. It was the secretary of a church.

"We need an interim pastor for several weeks. Would you be able to help us?"

"I would be very interested," Norman replied, "but I can't leave home just now. My wife is recuperating from a bad attack of sciatica and I need to be with her."

"We'd like you both to come," the man insisted.

Should they risk it? What if the crippling pain came back again and Amy just lay around, a liability in a strange place, and taking up Norman's time which should be given to the large congregation? As they prayed, a sense of certainty grew in their hearts. "This is My job for you. Go, and trust Me."

"Can't" had been buried. By faith they went to Christchurch.

On their return, Amy paid a final visit to the specialist. He asked her kindly how she was.

"I'm quite better, thanks."

"I should hardly think that is possible," he said sceptically but, to his amazement, it was. Then as she left, he warned, "These things can sometimes recur, you know!" But, in the mercy of God, there has been no recurrence.

When it became known that the McIntoshes were available to supply pastorless churches, requests came from far and near. In all, they took temporary pastorates in eleven churches of differing denominations from Auckland to Stewart Island. Not only was their contribution warmly welcomed, but their own lives were enriched by many new friendships.

Amy's job description for retirement included being on the panel of speakers for the Christian Women's Conventions International. She, who in her younger days couldn't abide women's meetings, found this service to women most satisfying and fruitful. It took her all over New Zealand.

For the first year or two after they moved to Invercargill, the Macs were more often away than at home. Gradually, however, they both began to long to stay put for a while. Only the Lord knew this feeling was in their hearts. Two things happened that brought them back home to stay.

While on their last pastorate, Amy discovered a lump where no lump should be. She chilled with apprehension. Could it be? The wait for the biopsy report seemed interminable. Whatever would she do if she had cancer?

She had. The growth was malignant and major surgery was ordered immediately. Fear threatened to overwhelm her, but as she cast herself into the arms of her heavenly Father, she felt herself cocooned in His love and her heart garrisoned with that peace which cannot be explained in human terms.

She went into the operation with the confidence that God was in control. The surgery was successful and she was spared the ordeal of follow-up therapy. In the six years since, there has been no recurrence of the disease.

The second thing that brought the Macs back home was an unexpected invitation for Norman to be chaplain to the Homes for the Elderly in Invercargill. Three homes are run by the Presbyterian Support Services for several hundred older folks. The ministry was advertized as "part-time," a description Norman subsequently found to be something of a misnomer!

He gave himself to these old people in his usual wholehearted fashion and they loved him. Many were only nominal Christians, and Norman's greatest desire was to bring them to a personal knowledge of the Saviour before they stepped out into eternity. His work brought him frequently to the bedsides of the sick and dying and into the company of the bereaved. Funerals provided a great opportunity to witness to the One who is victorious over death.

These were full, busy years. Norman was always in demand as a speaker. He loved to preach and was as welcome at youth meetings as he was in the pulpit. Amy produced radio scripts for the Far East Broadcasting Company, contributed articles for the women's section of the *NZ Challenge Weekly* and wrote regularly for the Religion and Life column of *The Southland Times*.

During retirement, there was more time than before for creative pursuits. For Norman this meant the fulfilment of a long-time dream, to have his own lathe and a workshop where he could do some creative woodwork. Wherever he went, he had an eye open for likely bits of wood that might be turned into beautiful bowls, dishes or lampstands.

Another ambition, apparently, was to be self-supporting in vegetables and to produce the earliest, largest and most prolific tomatoes in Southland! And so, life gradually settled into a satisfying and peaceful routine.

There was no premonition of disaster as Norman and Amy set off for the evening service one Sunday in January 1978. Only 24 hours earlier, Averil and her husband, Alan Bennett, with their four children had arrived from Thailand on leave, and they were all anticipating a happy few days together.

Thinking that the children might be feeling a bit strange, Averil stayed at home to get them to bed. Being midsummer, it was still light when Norman, Amy and Alan sauntered home after church. As they neared the house, they saw Averil at the gate obviously very distressed.

"Whatever is it?" they asked anxiously.

"It's Twink!" she gasped. They had all been awaiting news from Thailand of the arrival of Twink's fourth child, due that weekend. Had something gone wrong?

"No," whispered Averil, "it's Becky and Adele as well." She wept, "They've been killed, twelve of them!" Amy threw her arm around her distraught daughter and they all hurried into the house. Bit by bit the story unfolded.

While Averil was waiting for them to come home, she had turned on the television for the news. With horror she heard that there had been a serious accident in Thailand involving a New Zealand woman, Iona Parry. She was almost paralyzed as people started phoning in for confirmation. This couldn't be happening. This couldn't be true. It must be some awful dream.

Then a call came from Auckland confirming that a group of OMFers in Thailand had been involved in a road accident. A heavy truck, its driver earlier seen drinking at the market, had smashed head-on into their mini-bus, killing twelve people instantly — five adults and seven children. Several others were injured. Unbelievably, Twink and her two little girls were among the dead.

Bryan had been on duty at the hospital so was not with the party. He'd had to put aside his own grief all that dark night while he operated to save the lives of the survivers. Not until much later was he able even to see the bodies of his wife and children. Several six-year-old boys, including Matthew, had just come back from their first term at Chefoo. They had been sitting on the back seat and so, apart from minor injuries, were spared.

As Norman and Amy with Alan and Averil stood dumbly weeping in the face of what God had allowed, there was knock at the front door. A couple from miles away stood there with tears running down their faces. In their hands was a large basket of baking to help with the influx of sympathizers who would visit during the following days.

While they were still standing there, the phone rang again. It was Bryan calling from Thailand. Even as he told Dad and Mother about what had happened, he was conscious of being wonderfully upheld by the power of God. Then he spoke to Alan who, as Superintendent of Central Thailand, was feeling terribly frustrated and useless being so far away during such an emergency.

Actually, the telegram from Thailand telling of the accident had been sent to the wrong address in Auckland, so New Zealand was 24 hours later than other countries in hearing the news. Bryan had been wondering why there had been no word from Invercargill.

Only a few days before, in Bangkok, the husbands had minded the children to let Averil and Twink have a day together, a wonderful day of fun and fellowship on a nearby island. Averil said, "Strangely, even then I had a feeling of finality about a day that would never be repeated."

The day immediately before her death, Twink wrote joyous letters to every member of the family, and these arrived later as a great comfort to us all. They were full of fun and expressed her usual concern for the interests of each one to whom she wrote.

Early on Monday morning, the phone rang at the Christian Leaders' Training College in Papua New Guinea. My husband, Keith, and I were helping out there for a year while waiting for visas to return to Asia.

"It's a call from New Zealand," said the operator. My heart lurched. Was something wrong with Dad or Mother?

"I've got sad news for you," said Mother in a voice I hardly recognized. "Twink and the little girls are with the Lord." Then, once again the dreadful details were told.

The shock was like a physical blow. I staggered out into the pineapple patch to weep. After a while, my small daughter came to find me. She touched me tentatively. "Mummy?" Her eyes were anxious. I swept her into my arms and hugged her convulsively. What a comfort she was!

Just such a comfort had Twink been to our parents. She had brought sunshine into their lives on so many occasions. As a little five-year-old, it was Twinkle who had been such a light in the black darkness of that year of detention in Communist China.

Later, when Dad wrote from the Philippines confessing how inadequate he felt for the demands made upon him, it was teenage Twink who sent him a handkerchief on which she'd embroidered in bright red thread, "I LOVE MY CHARLIE BROWN!" This was followed up by postcards and letters of cheer to "My dear Charlie Brown."

More recently still, it was Twink again, always so loving, generous and optimistic who had done so much to help Dad and Mother through the painful days of readjustment to New Zealand and had supported Dad as he assumed his role as OMF Director.

As I remembered these things, I thought how deep would

be their grief. How helpless they would feel to be so far away, unable to do anything tangible to express their love for Bryan and Matthew. If only they could go to Thailand, but how could they ever manage it?

Then the Lord showed His hand. The employees of Air New Zealand were allowed generous concessions on airfares for their holidays. They were also permitted to take a relative with them at the same rate. Because it was an emergency, Lesley was able to take immediate leave, and within a day of receiving the news, she and Dad were on their way to Bangkok to attend the funeral.

In Thailand, OMFers were still reeling with shock when they arrived. Around the common grave, they were knit together in love and grief as they watched the bodies of the twelve laid to rest. Even as they wept, they affirmed their confidence in the One who would bring good out of evil, triumph out of tragedy and life out of death. This death would be to the glory of God.

But, in the meantime, there was the anguish of loss to be endured. After the funeral, Norman went on to Manorom where the whole community was in deep mourning. There, with Bryan and other bereaved parents, he wept and suffered. They encouraged one another to hope in the Lord, and their testimony was such that the unbelieving Thai looked on in amazement. "What kind of religion is Christianity, that people can face death like this? We have never seen anything like it."

Dr Julia Brown had been seriously injured in the accident and lay in traction. Her anxious mother, who was not a Christian, had flown out from Wales to be with her. Norman had the joy, even in the midst of pain, of leading her to the Saviour and seeing her completely transformed.

In different ways the Lord ministered to the bereaved. To Norman, he spoke His word of comfort through Proverbs 4:18. "But the path of the righteous is like the dawn, which shines brighter and brighter until full day." Twink had radiated light and love and laughter. Her life had been like the brightening dawn and now she was rejoicing in the full light of day. Her little daughters would never know the sorrows of life on earth.

I see heaven opened, thought Norman. *Soon we'll all be there together. Praise God for this certain hope.*

Back home in Invercargill, Amy was suddenly left alone. Yet she was not alone. The presence of the Lord filled the house and His strengthening word to her soul was, "Be concerned above everything else with the kingdom of God and with what I require of you . . . Look at Twink's death in the light of eternity and don't allow yourself to wallow in grief. There is the shadow of death, but My trusting child will *walk through* it. There is the Valley of Baca (weeping), but My believing child will *pass through* it. Trust Me for Twink and Bryan. As for you, you must go on — on to finish your course. Keep your eyes fixed on Me."

Still the thought persisted that Twink's death had been premature, a frightful waste, some sort of ghastly mistake. A few days later came further confirmation that there was no mistake. It was from Matthew 11. God's ways are often hidden from men. Even the wise and learned have no answers for many of the things that happen to God's servants. But those with the clear-eyed trust of little children are able to say, "Yes, Father, this was the way You wanted it."

The moulding and perfecting of the saints goes on to the end of life. Through this sorrow both Norman and Amy have entered into a more intimate communion with their Lord and they find a new capacity to comfort others who grieve.

The Bible speaks of sons as a "heritage" from the Lord and children being a "reward" from Him (Psalm 127:3). Norman and Amy have always felt very rewarded in their children and grateful for the gift of each one. While Alastair and Lesley have pursued interesting careers at home, Gavin, after some years as a student worker in New Zealand, went with his family to India under the auspices of the Bible and Medical Missionary Fellowship. Averil, Twink and I joined OMF for service in South East Asia.

Dad and Mother never prayed that their children would become missionaries, nor specifically dedicated us to that end. Their only concern was that we should come to know the Lord as Saviour and follow Him as Master. But they felt greatly honoured that God should have called four of us into the same service.

That we did so was by no means "inevitable." On the contrary, like most missionaries' children we were not so eager to follow in our parents' footsteps and would rather have carved out a life and identity of our own. So each one of us, in different ways, had to go through some fierce struggles before we were able to accept this as the "good and acceptable" will of the Lord for our own lives.

Throughout our years as missionaries, Dad and Mother have, not unnaturally, been our greatest and most understanding supporters. Once we may have resented our fancied loss of personal identity because of our relationship to such well-known parents. Now we rejoice in the very special privilege it is to have parents to whom we can "tell it all" because they have walked where we walk. Our identification with them as missionaries is a very precious and close bond over and above the love of family.

Having missionary children, however, means continued long separations. The sacrifice goes on into old age. Norman and Amy are very glad to have Alastair and his family close by and enjoy periodic visits from Lesley, but they miss the rest of us acutely.

During the four years following Twink's death they didn't see me or my family. So when, in 1982, they heard that Keith and I would have to forego our normal furlough to do post-graduate studies in the USA, they were extremely disappointed. This meant that we would have to return directly to our work at the Singapore Bible College and they could not expect to see us or our children for ten years.

The Lord, knowing how heavy-hearted they were about it, prepared a lovely surprise for them.

One day, while on assignment away from home, they

called to visit a man and his wife who, because of increasing years, could not get about as much as before. As they chatted and answered his questions about the family, they mentioned how much they missed seeing me.

Gently, he asked, "Would you like to see her?" They secretly thought it rather a superfluous question, but made some light remark and passed it off.

A few days later, the phone rang. It was a long-distance call from this friend. Without any preamble, he said quietly, "Well, you can go ahead and make those bookings for Los Angeles now. Tell Norman to come and get the money!"

Amy stood rooted to the floor. Such things happened to other people. Their own needs had always been met, but this was so much more. It was God's pleasure to grant them this desire and, in the process, to use them to minister to people in the USA.

Not only were they able to spend a real "family" Christmas and New Year with us in Pasadena, but they travelled in Florida, North Carolina, Colorado, Berkeley and South California as well, renewing acquaintance with a number of old friends and speaking at many meetings. It was a particular joy for them to share in the ongoing outreach of friends from their Philippine days with whom they had ministered in the Overseas Christian Servicemen's Centers. Another heart-warming experience was to spend Thanksgiving with Ed and Helen Spahr whom they had never thought to see again.

They had planned to leave a gift of $100 with us when they departed again for New Zealand, but there had been unexpected costs and they didn't have anything left. Just as Dad was putting on his coat to leave for the Los Angeles airport, he reached to put his travel papers into an inside pocket. There was something there. Surprised, for he hadn't used this pocket on his travels, he drew out an envelope on which was written, "Especially for you!" In absolute astonishment, he pulled out $100! He had no idea where it came from but our heavenly Father knew and had made provision. So they were able to make their gift after all!

As Norman and Amy press on to finish their course, they are often delighted by the unexpected discovery of fruit that has come from earlier sowing. Norman frequently meets up with pastors and missionaries who have gone forward to serve the Lord as a result of some message he has given. "I am in the ministry," a pastor told him recently, "because of a message you gave in our country valley when my brother and I were young."

Many folk have testified to blessing received when they learned how to give of their means to the Lord. Norman's oft-quoted remark, "You can't be right with God spiritually if you aren't right with Him financially," has brought conviction to many. Years before one young lady had responded with a bright, "Yes, Mac, what you say is true. When I gave the Lord a tenth, He so blessed me that now I give Him a twentieth!" Clearly her devotion was stronger than her mathematics.

At one convention for women, Amy's roommate greeted her with, "Do you remember me? I was in your 'keenite' class at Brown's Bay Children's Special Service Mission, and came to the Lord then." Forty years previously, and Amy had known nothing of it! At another conference where Amy was the speaker, the chairwoman turned to her and said, "I came to the Lord in your Crusader class at Gore High School." Again she had never known.

Wherever Norman and Amy have gone in life, they have particularly asked the Lord to give them friends, and he has done so. High on the list of those near and dear to them are their prayer partners and supporters who have faithfully, and often sacrificially, shouldered the load with them through many years. Loved missionary colleagues have brought them joy in every place. Friends of today, young and old, continue to put sparkle into life and encourage them to keep on faithful and obedient to the end. What would life be without them?

With joy and deep gratitude to the Lord, they look back over a lifetime in the royal service. When, at the beginning of their missionary career, they buried the word "can't" they gave God the opportunity to do great things through them. This He did, and in so doing has brought glory to Himself.

"Led by the Lord, they were as sure-footed as wild horses, and never stumbled. As cattle are led into a fertile valley, so the Lord gave his people rest. *He led his people and brought honour to his name*" (Isaiah 63:13,14 TEV).

Not long after the McIntoshes arrived home from China in 1943, Amy was asked to speak at a women's meeting.

The request was specific. "Please," they asked, "would you share with us some of your experiences?"

She was reluctant to do so because, when she recalled the harrowing events of the previous few years, she usually ended up having a sleepless night. As it was, too many things triggered off nervous reactions. For instance, the initial whirr of the Hanzhong air raid siren was identical with that of the Dunedin Town Hall clock. If either she or Norman happened to be in the vicinity when it started to strike the hour, they would instinctively "freeze" to the pavement.

However, these kindly ladies were insistent. So Amy opened up her heart and shared with them many details. While a good number of her hearers were stirred to action, one sprightly lady spoke to her at the door as she went out.

"Oh well, dear," she said comfortably, "it's the life you've chosen!" She drew her expensive fur coat around her shoulders and departed.

The remark stung. How little she understood. God had chosen their life — *they* had chosen to obey.

Amy turned to the Lord. "Master, You understand our hearts," she cried. "You know we wouldn't have it any other way!"

COURAGE

Our greatest need today, O Lord,
Resting in Thee and Thy sure Word,
Is courage straight from God's dear Son
Standing fast when all is done.

Not the courage of iron nerves,
Thou alone knowest our small reserves
To meet cruel, baffling cares that beat
Our timid spirits to fever heat.

Common bravery known of old,
Which past experience doth make bold,
Is not the courage of God's dear Son
Standing fast when all is done.

But courage that tears the binding yoke,
Refusing all fears that cling and choke,
Enervate and stultify,
This courage, Lord, O multiply!

When the weary months seem long,
Give us Thy triumphant song,
Victorious courage from God's dear Son
Standing fast when all is done.

Amy B. McIntosh

(Written while under detention in Communist China 1951)

"I have become absolutely convinced that neither Death
nor Life, neither messenger of heaven nor monarch of earth,
neither what happens today nor what may happen tomorrow,
neither a power from on high nor a power from below, nor
anything else in God's whole world has any power to separate
us from the love of God in Jesus Christ our Lord!"

Romans 8:38ff (Phillips)

MORE HELPFUL BIOGRAPHIES
FROM OMF BOOKS

TO A DIFFERENT DRUM
Why had Pauline Hamilton chosen to march to a different drum from her contemporaries, to experience danger and hardship in China and then Taiwan rather than security and prosperity in the USA?

Only because the God who had saved her from suicide and given meaning to her life had called, and as she obeyed she found Him faithful beyond all expectation.

BIOGRAPHY OF JAMES HUDSON TAYLOR
The classic story of the founder of the China Inland Mission (now OMF). Full of challenges to faith.

DOUG – MAN AND MISSIONARY
"... I think that someone in this meeting is called to the mission field", said the old deacon. I opened one eye and looked around at the assembled company. I couldn't see any of those ladies going to the mission field because they had husbands and families and maybe grandchildren to look after. On the other hand, I wasn't doing anything special...

So began Doug Abraham's missionary career. With cheerful London humour and warm commitment he tells his life story from early struggles and rebellions through thirty years of missionary service in Japan.